Hidden Steps
– BEHIND THE VEIL –

V. Nicholas Gerasimou

ISBN: 0692235159
ISBN-13:9780692235157

DEDICATION

To Dean; I couldn't have asked for a better partner to slug it out through our dysfunctional childhood with. Thick, thicker and thickest. I don't say it enough, I love you little brother.

CONTENTS

ACKNOWLEDGMENTS

I would like to thank all of you who have been with me on my walk with the Lord. To those of you who were there when it began, to those who are walking with me now, and to those who will be walking with me when my time on this Earth ends. I hope you all know how much you mean to me.

In his heart a man plans his course,
but the Lord determines his steps.
(Proverbs 16:9)

V. Nicholas Gerasimou

PREFACE

How random, is random? How much chance is actually involved in chance? We move through our days feeling confident that we've got a pretty good grasp on what makes real, real... and what makes gambling a cosmic roll of the dice. Many people plow ahead believing they make their own destiny, and sometimes things just happen. Well, that may be true to an extent, but I think the bigger question is; why am I here?

Well, that is THE question isn't it? What's my purpose? What *is* the meaning of life? When you boil the theology, existential ponderings, and religiosity down to the marrow, you come to one clarifying, polarizing question. What do I believe in?

Whether it be in an all knowing, all powerful, omnipotent sovereign God; or as the many patrons of the casinos in Las Vegas would attest to, the presence or absence of the all powerful "*Lady Luck*".

Gambling aside, as far as this author can tell, the only way for a skeptic of the "Divine Plan" ideology can find out for sure, is to leave this world and see what happens. The obvious flaw in that plan is that once they find out, they can't come back and tell anybody about what they discovered, one way or another.

Through my own meandering journey through this world so far, I have seen a good deal of outlandish and amazing things, been in a number of situations I've had trouble explaining, and survived a small handful of experiences that I should not have.

I could subscribe to "*Lady Luck*" and her alluring call that I may just get lucky one day; and to this point in my life that's exactly what I've done.

Hopefully the story of Conner and the few dramatic and at times graphic snapshots of his life, as well as the unseen spiritual warfare which I believe is going on all around us, will help give anyone who rides with *"Lady Luck"* a new perspective on destiny. As for this author... I choose faith.

CHAPTER 1

THE JOY OF JOY

V. Nicholas Gerasimou

THE JOY OF JOY

"Con, what's up man?" Dave plopped down on the couch next to Connor and kicked his feet up on the worn coffee table. It was covered in what most bachelor-esque, college apartment coffee tables should be covered with. Strange off-colored stains told stories of late night food runs greedily inhaled in front of the television. Cans of every sort, formed a kind of miniature alcoholic Stonehenge, where at the moment the remote control was playing the part of the sacrificial alter.

"Nothin', sup with you?" Conner replied.

"Nothin'," Dave shot back.

The two sat in silence for a few moments.

Dave lazily rolled his head to face Conner and said, "So… I don't think I'm going to class today."

"Which one?" Conner asked.

"Any of em'," Dave said matter-of-factly.

Conner thought about it for a moment then nodded to himself, "I'm in. I've got Econ at," he looked at his watch and sighed, "fifteen minutes ago, and I really don't feel like listening to how the macro makes the micro go boom."

"That doesn't make any sense," Dave said after a few seconds.

"Your face doesn't make any sense. What do you want to

do?" Conner asked.

"Well… we could drink. Go to the pool?"

"Dude, it's sixty degrees out and it's nine-thirty in the morning." Conner flatly replied.

Dave shrugged, "So, no pool then?"

Conner closed his eyes and spoke through a yawn, "We drank last night. I think my liver is going to give it's two week notice."

Dave reached out and slapped Conner hard across the cheek like he was challenging him to a duel, "How dare you sir?"

Conner blinked hard as he let the warm sting subside and then turned to face Dave, "Seriously?"

"Look. You need to reassess your priorities," Dave said with a finger wagging in Conner's face like a metronome. "When else in our lives will we have no responsibilities? When else will it be considered socially acceptable to drink and do nothing at ten in the morning ever again? Answer Me Damn-it!"

Conner studied his feet for a few moments, then jumped up off of the couch and slapped his thighs with both hands, "I'm in."

"Yes!" Dave popped up to his feet and raised a hand for a celebratory high five.

Conner smiled and cracked Dave hard across his right cheek with an open hand. "You earned that."

Dave blinked and his eyes watered, "Agreed." He looked to the kitchen, "Do we have anything left after last night?"

Conner shrugged, "Not sure. Joe drinks it by the gallon and he didn't leave until when?"

"Two-thirty? Three in the morning?" Dave offered.

"Nose goes!" Conner blurted. Recognition flashed across Dave's face but it was too late. Conner had shot the tip of his pointer finger to the tip of his nose.

"Lame." Dave shouldered passed Conner and made his way to the kitchen.

Conner sat back down and took in the room, "We should

clean at some point." For what they paid per month the apartment itself wasn't bad. It was decently sized and gave them plenty of room to entertain, which they did with regularity. A twenty-by-twenty living room served as the common gathering area for the two. Pieces of hand-me-down furniture had been opportunistically scavenged, and had become a part of the landscape over the last two years. Spots marked the carpets and scuffs and scratches lined the walls. A poster of three bikini clad beer girls covered a person sized hole near the television where a friend had decided to play "fly on a windshield" one drunken night. It was dirty, it was beat-up, but it was college and it was home.

"Out," came Dave's voice from the kitchen.

"Nose still goes dude," Conner called back toward Dave.

Dave came walking out of the kitchen toward the front door, "I'll go get a case and some snacks but you gotta pick up around here."

"Done. And done. And get some of those chili-lime chips," said Conner. "They're goooood."

Dave cracked the door, stepped outside and took a deep breath, "Extra thick this morning."

"Great," Conner called back.

A misty brown haze hung over the San Bernardino Valley and had almost completely blanketed out the mountain range to the west. Smog, along with a good number of other life adjustments had become commonplace for the two boys since they moved from the affluent suburbs on the coast, inland to go to school and play football.

The University of Redlands was a beautiful school, filled with privileged children from across the nation who wanted a small school environment. Those students lived on campus in safe, happy, clean, well-lit dormitories. They ate in cafeterias and never saw anything but what the University wanted them to see. The college experience.

Unfortunately that experience cost a great deal of money. Money which Conner and Dave didn't have. Instead of a homogenous, hermetically sealed bubble of upper-middle-class safety, the two friends were forced to live a few miles from campus on the South-West side.

Low rent housing and crime were the norm for the two. From what they could deduce, for blocks in either direction, they were the only people living in the Valley Crest Apartment Complex who did not have some type of criminal enterprise, violent tendency, drug related problem, or gang affiliation.

Eighteen months of being lulled to sleep by the sounds of their neighbors flirting with domestic violence, and being awakened by police sirens, had calloused the friends to the reality of life in the projects. At that point they just looked at it as a part of their everyday grind.

As Dave crunched down the dried grass in front of their apartment to the street where his van was parked, a white Honda Accord pulled up and parked in front of him. Conner pulled back the blinds with a hooked finger, and craned his neck from his spot on the couch to see who it was.

"Awww, Crap… it's Joy." He rolled his eyes and with an exasperated flick, let the blinds flap back into place.

Ω

Dave had been dating Joy for about two months, and that was a month and three weeks too long if you asked Conner. The two had met one lazy Saturday night at a local bar dubbed The Dirty Bird. The Flamingo if you were an out-of-towner. From what Conner could tell it was a relationship founded on the unshakeable pillars of mutual sexual attraction and alcohol.

For some reason he didn't see wedding bells, a dog and two-point-five happy, rosy-cheeked children in the couples' future. But that didn't matter at the moment because Dave was in lust with her, and it seemed she was a semi-permanent fixture in his life.

Conner got up and walked to the front door. He watched her slither from the driver's seat of her car (the way she walked, there was no other way to describe it. She seemed to saunter... sashay... no, she slithered) up to Dave and attempt to crawl into his soul through his mouth. Conner thought about yelling at them to get a room but at the moment he thought perhaps a bank vault, or a nuclear silo bunker; maybe the bottom of the ocean would be a more appropriate place to hide their unbridled passion for each other.

He considered the latter option for a moment; the two of them locked in a boa constrictor embrace at the bottom of the Marianas Trench. How would he get them there? Duct tape or rope? He'd have to get some type of weight to get them to sink... maybe an anvil like in the cartoons. But how would he get all of them into the back of his truck; and where does one find an anvil for that matter? It's not like they sell them at Home Depot.

A barking dog across the street snapped him out of his macabre daydream. He shook it off and headed down the hall to his room. So much for his relaxing morning of beer and chili-lime flavored chips. He loved those chips. In one motion he fell on his bed grabbed the TV remote and switched on his desk fan.

Ω

"Hey Con?" Dave called back into the apartment.

Conner hit mute on the TV remote, "So, how bout that ice cold beer? Mmmmm, sounds real good about now."

Dave walked into the room and leaned against the doorjamb, "Dude, we need to talk."

Conner laid his head back on his pillow and stared at the ceiling, "Here's the thing, if it doesn't have to do with an alcoholic beverage in my hand or artificially flavored chips in my mouth... I don't really care."

Dave stood silently by the door and waited. Conner could feel his friend's expectant eyes laying heavy on the side of his face.

"What?" Conner finally yelled, his frustration evident.

Dave took that as a sign indicating his temporary room banishment had ended. He sat down on the edge of Conner's bed. "So what are you doing right now?"

Conner looked around the room, at the remote in his hand, then at the TV, "Well; what does it look like?" Before Dave could formulate an answer he fired off a quick jab laced with sarcasm, "How's Joy?"

"Good," Dave ran a nervous hand through his hair, "She's actually what I came in here to talk to you about." Conner's perfect morning was getting less perfect by the minute.

Ω

Dave laid out a sob story heavy with hypotheticals and hyperbole. Apparently in the past, Joy may or may not have dated someone. That someone may have been involved in a loosely networked and unregulated pharmaceutical sale and distribution enterprise.

"So he's a drug dealer?" Conner said flatly.

"Well... he..." Dave's sentence got stuck in his throat.

"Dude! Don't B.S me...." Conner said.

Dave counted on his fingers, "Okay yes, but it's not that bad. He sells a little Pot, and some Coke," Conner raised his eyebrows and cocked his head in an expectant look, "and I think Joy said he may move some ecstasy... and she said he got popped for meth a few years back."

Conner swung his legs over the side of the bed and sat up, "In what backwards, idiotic, dumb-ass, naive universe is that, *not that bad?*"

Dave shrugged, "He's just a normal run-of-the-mill scum-bag guy. That's all."

Conner shook his head and rubbed his eyes with his palms, "Freakin' Pablo Escobar," He looked up at Dave, "So what does she want from us?"

The more Dave talked, the less Conner liked where his morning was headed. Apparently when things turned sour for the star-crossed lovers, Joy left their communal drug nest and went to stay with a friend. While Joy was staying at "*said friend's*" apartment, there was a break-in.

"So?" Conner asked, "She lives off Orange Street, there are break-in's over there all the time."

Dave shook his head, "Nah man, it's what they took. What *he* took, and how he took it. No broken windows, no kicked in doors. Total stealth."

We'll just say that Joy used to keep large sums of money in the form of loose cash (mostly tens and twenties) in a small, dented tin box with a picture of the Cookie Monster on the lid. The box was then rolled inside a pair of purple sweat pants, and hidden under her bed.

"How much?" Conner asked.

"She said about twenty-five hundred bucks... give or take."

"She ever heard of a bank?"

Dave shrugged again, "She said she was about to put a deposit down on a new apartment and buy a few things for her place."

"Mmm-Hmm. Where'd she get it?" Asked Conner.

"She's a server down at Chili's," Dave motioned over his shoulder like it was down the hall.

"Ser-vi-cer's more like it," Conner mumbled under his breath.

Dave punched him hard enough in the shoulder to make him wince, "Still my girlfriend, ass-clown. Easy with that stuff."

Conner put his hands up in a mock show of surrender. "Okay, so I'm still waiting for the punch line to this screwed up joke you're telling."

"No joke. She says her ex stole her money and she wants us to go with her when she gets it back."

Conner stared at the floor for a few seconds then looked at Dave, "How did her ex know where the money was if she had moved to her friend's apartment on a whim?" He shook his head as the tumblers in his mind fell into place, "She said she moved out after they broke up. She said things got bad."

He raised his eyebrows quizzically, "Physical?"

Dave pursed his lips and nodded in affirmation.

Conner picked up where he left off, "So, why would she tell her ex, who put hands on her, whom she broke up with... where she moved to and *exactly* where she kept two thousand bucks in cash?" He shook his head again, "Doesn't make any sense dude. How would he have known to look there; *and* who is this guy, Daniel Ocean? How does he get in and out with no forced entry or anyone seeing him?" Conner stared at Dave and waited expectantly for a reply.

Dave exhaled in exasperation, "Maybe she always kept stuff under her bed and he knew to look there."

"That," Conner poked Dave in the forehead with his index finger, "Is the stupidest thing I've ever heard. And you," A second thump from Conner made Dave blink, "are a moron if you believe that."

Dave fluttered his hand in front of his face like he was trying to shoo away the assaulting finger as if it was a curious fly, "Look, she said that they had been talking on the phone. Trying to reconcile and stuff, and he had come over once." The look that Conner shot at Dave was a double barrel blast of disgust.

"No, no no... *Before* she and I hooked up. Anyway, she said he had threatened her, and demanded that she owed him money for something."

Conner broke in, "For what?"

"Not sure," Dave answered, "she didn't say. But she said he was lying."

"Well of course he was. Why wouldn't he be?" Conner said, the sarcasm almost palpable. "This just seems wrong dude. Off."

"Conner, please. I need your help. She just wants us to go with her to talk to her ex. Just help her get it back"

Conner threw up his arms like a referee signaling a game winning field goal that had just skimmed inside the left upright, "What does she want us to do? Steal it back?" He thumbed his chest, "I'm not a goon in a mobster movie."

Dave sat silent for a second, then looked up at Conner, "Well... would you just come for me? Just for like, moral support. You don't have to do anything; just stand there and look tough and handsome." He smiled and nudged Conner with an elbow, "Come on Con, I doubt there will be any drama. She just wants to talk to him. Reason with him."

Conner's shoulders slumped. His perfect morning had just jumped the tracks and was careening down the mountain toward the village at the bottom. Conner was pretty sure the villagers were doomed.

Ω

The three sat in the living room; Dave and Joy on the couch by the front window cuddled and talked, while Conner sat across the room with his arms crossed. He studied them more than he looked at them. Like Jane Goodall watching the mating habits of Silverback Gorillas. He should have been taking notes. The possible scenarios for the next hour of his life played over and over in his head like a song when you forget to uncheck the repeat tab. The more he thought about it, the angrier he became.

"Thanks for helping me out Conner," said Joy.

Conner snapped out of his mental wrestling match and jumped back into the moment, "Hey, no problem Joy. Just hope we can help find out who took your money, or get it back, or... like I said, no problem."

She smiled and ran her hand through Dave's hair. Conner smiled back, and really had to concentrate on it not looking like a scowl. She was attractive. Not in the traditional, cute, sweet, good bone structure kind of a way; but in the hard biker-princess wearing a bikini and leather boots, with the naughty body you see on the web-sites you shouldn't be looking at, kind of a way. He could see where his best friend's enthusiasm for this girl came from. They were in trouble.

Ω

The bubble of silence the three were sitting in popped abruptly. It was like a water-buffalo somersaulting through a stemware display case when Joe came bursting through the front door, "Hey-heyyyy! Who needs their skull crushed?" Conner raised his hand and sarcastically pointed to the crown of his head with an index finger.

"Hey Joe," Conner wiggled his raised fingers in a lazy wave. Joe pointed the baseball bat he had in his left hand at Conner and smiled. Dave and Joy said hello as Joe fell onto the couch next to Conner. "Sup man?" Joe asked.

Conner smacked his lips, "Nada. Sup with you bud?"

Joe could be an intimidating person if you didn't know him. Honestly, Joe was pretty intimidating even if you did know him. Conner was willing to bet the guy's own mother was a little afraid of him. Every inch of his six-four frame was packed with layer upon layer of hormone-aided muscle. Joe was two-hundred and forty pounds of bulging, vein-popping, mentally unstable human being, whom at the moment was twirling an aluminum baseball bat between two fingers like it was a drum-major's baton. He made for a great defensive lineman, and a good guy to have with you, when going to steal two-grand from a mid-level drug dealer with your best friend and his ex-stripper girlfriend.

Dave looked up at Conner, "Manny should be here soon, then we'll head out."

"Great…" Came Conner's flat reply.

Ω

Dave's van was messier than usual. Food wrappers, crumpled papers, moist gym clothes and an eclectic menagerie of other filth covered the interior of the slowly dying automobile. Dave drove, Joy sat to his right and Conner, Joe and Manny had to excavate little areas of open space to sit in the back.

Joy nervously chewed on her thumbnail as she mumbled directions to Dave. Joe and Manny quipped about a "rumble" and doused each other in bravado as Conner stewed. His stomach had gone from practicing gymnastics to a full-blown Grand-mal seizure. Something kept telling him that this was a bad idea. It all just felt wrong, and he didn't want to admit it, but he was scared.

Before he could think about why, he whispered a silent prayer under his breath like he was talking to an old friend. "God... please get us out of this. Keep us safe. This is so bad," He looked up at Joy and his eyes narrowed, "Jesus just watch over us and get us home in one piece. Thanks."

"Huh?" Joe asked, "You say somethin'?"

"Nah man. Just humming to myself," It gave Conner pause that he was talking to God. He couldn't remember praying for much of anything since he stopped going to church in high school. Like God would listen to him now. Wasn't there like a statute of limitations on being protected by God if you didn't go to church? But to his surprise he continued to pray until they pulled up and parked next to the side gate of Joy's ex-boyfriend's complex.

They piled out of the van and all looked at the fence. Joe spoke first, "So, do we hop it?"

"You can. I personally don't feel like getting a four-inch spike up my ass," Conner said, referring to the ornate metalwork at the top of each spire on the fence.

Joe looked over at Manny, "Can't you get over it? Isn't that how your family got here in the first place?"

Joe laughed when Manny threw a punch into his ribs, "My dad was born in Irvine, jerk. I don't even speak Spanish."

"Take it easy little buddy. Kidding," Joe said with a smile.

Conner snapped, "Will you two shut the hell up?!" The uneasiness that had been welling in him spilled over into full-blown paranoia. He had a gray hooded sweatshirt on but couldn't stop shivering.

Ω

Rap music: actually it was the bone-shaking thud of the base cannon in the trunk of the lowered black Cadillac that got everyone's attention. Conner could feel the concussion shock waves ripple his jeans against the skin on his shins, from thirty feet away.

The windows were tinted a midnight black. Manny, Conner and Joe just looked from the car to each other, and back to the car. The driver's side window slowly slid down and a large, black muscular arm draped down the door like a slab of beef. The man inside had on a large pair of sunglasses that covered most of his face. He reached up, pulled the cigarette out of the corner of his mouth and blew a mushroom cloud of smoke toward the group by the gate.

Conner pulled his face back with a look of mild confusion. The man in the Caddy pulled out a cell phone, said a few words, gave the group by the gate another long-hard look, then slowly drove away.

"Tell me you saw that Joe," Conner pleaded.

"Oh I saw it," Joe replied.

"This is so screwed."

Ω

"You did what!" Conner screamed. Dave had to step in between Joy and his best friend to keep him off of her. "Are you insane? Hey I know… why don't we just put up a huge banner, or hire a plane to skywrite that we're on our way?"

"Hire a marching band?" Manny offered from behind them. Conner turned and pointed at him in agreement.

"Don't you mean a Mariachi band?" Joe added.

Manny took a deep breath, "Seriously… I hate you."

Conner turned back to Joy, "Actually, *None* of that would have been as bad as calling him, and telling him we were coming." He turned away in disgust.

Dave walked up behind his friend and put a hand on his shoulder, "Hey, it doesn't matter. We are only here to talk. No drama. Remember?"

Conner turned back and looked at Dave, "It just feels wrong man. This is a bad idea. It just feels like she's setting us up."

"For what?" Dave asked. "Setting us up for what? What does that even mean?" Before Conner could answer everyone stopped and looked toward the sidewalk gate; it was buzzing.

Ω

Joe and Connor trailed behind Manny, Dave and Joy.

"Joe… why would he buzz us in? Think about it. I mean… come on; would you buzz your crazy ex-girlfriend in with an entourage of four guys she brought with her, to potentially kick your ass and take money from you?"

"I don't know Con. But that's what this baby is for," He twirled the shiny aluminum bat in his hands.

"You are not helping Joe." Conner said. Joe just smiled.

Ω

"It's up these stairs, apartment 4b." Joy said as she pointed to the nearest flight. She seemed more nervous than before. The nails on her right hand were chewed down to the quick, and she had started the process on the other hand.

Conner walked up behind Dave and grabbed him by the back of the shirt, "If this turns or gets weird, we are outta here. You hear me? Gonzo."

"Alright just relax. It's gonna be fine," Dave said as he started up the stairs. Joy reached the door first and waited for Dave to reach the top before she knocked. Joe, Manny and Connor stood behind them on the landing and waited.

Conner's heart was racing. He had to calm down. The wood was rough under his palms as he leaned on the railing of the porch landing. It needed a new coat of paint. *Breathe… just breathe*. The mantra repeated in his head as he looked out and surveyed the complex. As an aside, it was nice. Quaint little streams lined with thousands of smooth black river stones, zigzagged their way across the entire property. Someone had done an admiral job convincing almost every tree and shrub to adhere to a strict dress code.

Most of the smog had blown off and a brisk afternoon breeze blew through the valley. The air tasted crisp on his tongue. It had turned into a beautiful day. He could see the suggestion of snow at the crest of the mountains to the West and he found himself imagining how easily he could be there right now.

He could just walk away. Not say a word. Ignore everyone when they asked where he was going. Just turn, walk down the stairs and out of the complex. Walk home, into his apartment, into his room, grab his car keys and be up in the mountains in an hour or two. Instead of waiting to see what was on the other side of the door Joy was knocking on, he could be walking around in the snow. He imagined listening to it crunch as it packed beneath his feet. Breathtaking vistas and smelling the fresh icy-cold… the monologue of his daydream was rudely cut off mid-sentence.

They all froze when the lock unlatched from inside. The door slowly creaked open about six inches and a slender face filled the crack. "Hey Joy," the face motioned with it's nose toward the four men standing behind her, "Who're they?"

Dave abruptly jumped in, adrenaline and bravado winning out over better judgment, "Dave. I'm Dave," he thumbed behind him, "That's Manny, Joe and Conner."

"Great genius, tell him our names." Conner whispered under his breath. Joe bounced on his toes with the bat hidden behind his left leg.

"Will you stand still?" Conner hissed with a nudge. Joe just smiled.

"I want my money Mike," Joy said as she placed her hand on the door and tried to push it open.

Mike put his foot against the bottom jamb to stop it, "Look, relax. Don't get uppity and make a scene. Stop this. You know I don't have your money," he pointed to the small valley of exposed flesh between her enhanced breasts, "Reason being you never had any to begin with you junkie bitch."

Dave's back tensed and Conner put a hand on his shoulder, "Easy," he whispered it like one would to a German Sheppard who had just seen a cat.

The two bickered for a minute or two, and testosterone once again won-out and hi-jacked Dave's brain, "Look Mike, quit jerking her around. Just give her the money so we can go. We don't want to be here either."

Mike stopped and slowly looked Dave up and down studying him. It was almost seductive. It was also very uncomfortable to watch. After a few seconds his eyes snapped up and locked on Dave's, "I don't know you and you obviously don't know me. Trust me little man, you're right. You do-not want to be here." He turned back to Joy, "Now if you'd like to come in and talk in a more civilized manner you're welcome to. Come on in."

As Mike moved aside and pulled the door open, Conner's stomach dropped. From where he was standing Conner could count about ten people lounging around inside the living room of the apartment. As Joy and Mike picked up their agitated dialogue another person strolled out of the hallway.

Conner spoke out of the side of his mouth, "This is over Joe, I'm pulling the plug." He positioned himself directly behind Dave when something caught his eye. A shimmer. It was the sun reflecting off of metal. The smooth chrome metal that made up the barrel of a gun. A gun that was stuffed into the belt of the angry looking man who had just sat down on the arm of the couch, and was now staring dead into Conner's eyes.

"Enough. That's it. We are gone." That's what Conner wanted to say. Unfortunately before he could utter the first word of their retreat, Joy was gone. She was in the middle of a string of very colorful and imaginative curse words, when she bolted into the apartment. Before Dave could react, the door slammed shut and the dead-bolt clunked into place.

"Joy!" Dave screamed as he began to pound on the door with closed fists. Raised voices and sounds of a struggle floated out to the group from behind the door. Conner and Joe just stared at each other; Conner in numb disbelief, Joe with excitement.

"What the hell just happened?" Conner asked in shocked wonder.

"This just got interesting," Joe said, a smile playing at the corner of his mouth.

"Joy!" Dave backed up, drew his knee to his chest, and started to level front-kicks next to the handle. The frame shook but the door held. Conner shut his eyes and balled his fists. All he wanted to do today was drink a beer or two, eat some chips, watch some TV and maybe get a bean-and-cheese burrito from that hole-in-the-wall place down on Orange St. Those things were amazing with that home-made salsa they ladled on top.

In mid-kick the door flew open and Joy came springing out. She was flushed and her shirt was torn; a puffy red hand print screamed from her left cheek.

"I'm gonna kill you!" Mike barked, holding a hand to a set of fresh claw marks that started at the bottom of his right ear, and disappeared beneath the collar of his shirt.

Joy popped the clutch, and shifted from hysterical to whatever emotion makes a person foam at the mouth while they vomit profanity.

"Kill *me*? KILL ME! I'll kill you and all your junkie tweaker friends!" Dave held her by the waist as she threw wild kicks and clawed hands with talon-like acrylics toward Mike's face.

Mike looked back into the apartment and held out an open hand as if to stay any of his agitated compatriots from reacting to Joy's venomous threats.

"Look," Mike closed his eyes for a moment, then they shot open, "Dave. Right?"

Dave nodded, "Dave."

"This girl you think you know doesn't exist. This," he pointed at the red, panting wolverine Dave had around the waist, "Is the real Joy. Ain't she though?"

"What?" Dave asked.

"A Joy," He looked down at her, "The Joy of Joy. That's what we all used to say huh boys?" He said with a smile. A chorus of muffled agreement floated from the apartment.

"This girl is using you bro. You're just a tool to her so she can get what she wants. My money."

"Liar!" The word slid through her clenched teeth like lava.

Dave had a moment of pause and began to truly assess the situation. He looked past Mike at the small army he had at his disposal then back at his three friends. Conflict was not the best course of action. "Joy, re-lax!" He shook her as he said it, "We are going to deal with all of this later."

Joy seemed to uncoil in Dave's arms. The tension left her back and her fists unfurled. "Fine… fine. Please put me down. I'm okay."

Dave gave Conner a *"Go Figure"* look and set her down. Everyone involved took the respite of peace to adjust. Shirts were straightened, faces were wiped with sleeves and Mike seemed to let his guard down. Joy regained her composure. She ran a hand through her wild hair and brushed at her pant-legs before she straightened up and faced him.

There was a moment of awkward silence. A car horn echoed off in the distance. Conner was very aware of his own breathing; it seemed very loud in his head for some reason.

The corner of Joy's mouth started to twitch. Mike's eyes narrowed then widened with recognition but it was too late. The twitch spread into an evil maniac grin. There was a dull thud when the flat of Joy's boot connected with Mike's crotch. As he fell, she jack-rabbited past Conner and Manny. She was almost at the bottom of the stairs when Mike hit the ground.

"Truck… my truck," Mike wheezed out between coughing fits.

The entire apartment jumped to it's collective feet in unison like the beginning to a flash-mob number.

The weight of the moment hit Conner first and he broke the trance, "Go!" He grabbed the back of Dave's shirt and yanked him toward the stairs. Manny and Joe followed suit. Thankfully a doorway is only so big and Mike was currently curled in the fetal position at the threshold, which bought them a few precious seconds.

Ω

Despite the heavy black boots Joy was wearing she seemed to float down the concrete path toward the parking lot. Conner, Joe, Manny and Dave followed close behind, with the entire population of apartment 4B bringing up the rear.

"She's a nimble little thing huh?" Joe panted out between breaths.

"Let's get Dave and get the hell outta here!" Conner yelled back. Joe nodded.

By the time the four reached the parking lot, Joy was busy. She danced around the sandstone gray, lifted truck with the chrome wheels, and kicked and punched and keyed with a truly energized vigor. It was almost manic.

"Joy! Stop!" Dave screamed.

"Screw him! He owes me!" She yelled back. That started a game of cat-and-mouse around Mike's truck.

A booming laugh erupted from behind them and Conner turned to see that Joe had doubled back and had faced the approaching mob. He was swinging the baseball bat in front of him, in wide looping arcs keeping the group at bay. He looked like a crazed lion tamer trying to train an entire pride.

"Joe! Enough!" He turned back to Dave, "We need to go!" Dave looked over at Conner, then beyond him to see some of the mob had filtered around Joe and were quickly on their way.

"Oh… dead. We're dead!" He made a move and lunged for Joy and caught her by the back of the jeans. With one forceful yank she was off the ground and tucked under his arm; his very own screaming, kicking duffle bag.

Conner heard the sharp scratch of rubber soles scuffing gravel over asphalt behind him. He spun just in time to see that Mike had recovered from his testicular trauma, made his way to the parking lot and was about four feet from him with rage in his eyes.

Mike lowered his shoulder and prepared to bowl through Conner. Luckily nine years of football had conditioned him to avoid, and without thinking he side-stepped the would-be battering ram like a matador. As Mike rolled past, Conner brought an expertly timed elbow down on his spine sending him chest first to the pavement. He exhaled profanity as he skidded to a stop.

Conner backed up trying to keep the growing group of people in his field of vision. Four people including Mike had arrived so far. A number of people had taken some pretty vicious tags from Joe's bat, but the sheer number of bodies overwhelmed him and he started to battle.

Mike pushed himself up and dusted off his shirt. He cracked his neck and looked at Dave, "I don't care about you or your friends. I want her."

Conner was about eight feet from the truck, five feet from Mike and three of his compatriots, and around twenty feet from where Joe had just wrapped the bat around someone's neck and was using them as a human shield. He had no idea where Manny was. Mike pointed a bleeding angry finger in Conner's direction without taking his eyes off of Dave and Joy, "You stay put hero. This ain't your beef."

Fire burned in his eyes, "You... I'm gonna kill you bitch." Mike said as he started toward the truck.

Conner made a move in his direction; just a quick step, "Hey..."

His stomach dropped as he saw. He went numb inside; like he was watching a movie of himself. As Conner made his move, Mike's tattooed partner caught him out of the corner of their eye. With a flip of his wrist the chrome 9mm had appeared from the waistband of his jeans and was drawing a line on Conner's heart.

It sparkled in the afternoon sun making Conner squint. It all happened so fast but at the same time seemed to take an eternity. Adrenaline dumped into Conner's veins. His heart punched at the inside of his ribs; he could feel the pulse in his throat. He drew in a long powerful breath and time froze. He heard birds up in the maple tree next to him having a conversation. About what, he wondered? Did they know what was happening below them? Would they care if they did? A cool breeze kissed his cheek; it smelled like fall. He wanted to be at home so badly. On the couch, watching TV eating those stupid chili-lime chips.

The gun just hung there in the air like a lazy metal balloon. Five feet. He could have almost reached out and touched the barrel. So close. A tingle ran up his spine and his eyes watered. He exhaled, then the world exploded in a flash and boom.

Ω

Everyone jumped when the sharp report echoed through the parking lot. Just one staccato pop. Conner fell and landed flat backed next to the truck. Everything just stopped. The fighting, the panic; even the birds took a moment to look down and see what all the fuss was about.

Dave let go of Joy and she fell to the pavement catching her head on the rim of the tire as she did.

Mike stood slack jawed for a moment and then frustration and anger washed over his face, "What the hell is WRONG with you?" He barked back to his accomplice. "Like we need this kind of heat right now!" He motioned to the apartment complex, "At my house!"

Dave yelled Conner's name and started around the front of the truck. The shooter bounced on his toes, eyes wide, almost frantic. He really couldn't believe that he'd actually shot someone. It just kind of happened. It had been a bad day. The shakes were getting pretty severe. It had been around eight hours since his last fix and his arm itched something fierce. He just stood there, bouncing and twitching. He felt like he was waiting, but waiting for what he didn't know. Maybe for the guy on the ground to get up, say he was okay. Maybe for Mike to tell him what to do. He really wanted someone to come on over and pop one into the vein on his biceps so he could calm down. So he stood there with the gun still pointed at Conner's motionless body and waited.

Dave came skidding around the hood of the truck. "Conner!"

Without thinking, Killian (that was his name, Killian) drew a line on the picture of a blue barreling wave that was on the middle center mass of Dave's tee-shirt. He started to pull back on the trigger.

Ω

Another shot echoed through the parking lot. Dave jumped as a smoking hole appeared next to him on the truck's left front quarter-panel. As Killian pitched forward, the softball sized rock that Manny had thrown at the back of his head rolled under the truck. A small piece of scalp was stuck to it like the peel on an orange.

Dave patted himself down from chest to groin and thanked God, 'He missed! Holy hell; did that just happen?"

"Thank God he's a lousy shot," Came Conner's voice. He was groggy and still laying on his back but he was alive.

"Con! You're okay!" Dave scooted over to his friend and helped him up to his feet. Conner was a bit woozy but managed to keep his balance. There was blood on the back of his head matting his hair down, but otherwise he was no worse for wear.

"Shot?" Dave asked as he looked for blood that should have been pouring out of a dime-sized hole in Conner's chest.

Conner lazily looked down and shook his head, which

hurt so he stopped, "No." He looked up at Dave, "No."

Everyone else in the parking lot looked on in a kind of dazed silence. Joe had let go of his human shield and now stood shoulder to shoulder with his attackers; no one seemed to notice.

"My truck!" Mike snapped back to life. "You shot my truck!" He looked down at Killian and fired a short kick into his ribs. "And you," he pointed at Joy who had stood up and was slowly backing away holding a hand to her head. "You're gonna pay for all of this. All of it! If I have to pass you around to my crew as a play toy, I'll charge by the hour until my truck is fixed."

"Enough," Conner had recovered enough to have a little confidence back in his voice. "I'm done, we're done," he looked over at Dave and then motioned to Manny to join them, "We are just going to leave. Joe…"

Joe slowly looked to his left, then rolled his head lazily to the right. Eight sets of very angry eyes fixed on him. "Gotta go!" Joe spat out as he sprinted to where Conner and Dave were standing.

Conner turned back to Mike and held out his arms in surrender, "Look, Mike. I don't care about any of this. I just want to take my friends and go home."

Mike motioned with his nose, "Then go. My beef is with little miss over there. We are going to have a long, long talk."

"She's coming with us," Dave immediately shot back. Manny had taken up a spot next to Conner and Joe was standing over by the truck and seemed to be examining the tire.

"You all got lucky today. Vegas lucky. That dumb bitch ain't worth it. She's poison, trust me. Take your little boy-band, cut your losses and leave. Leave her to me." As he finished, a wry smile spread across his face and he held his arms out to the group of men who had gathered behind him. "What're you gonna do anyway? You're still a tad bit outnumbered."

"This," came Joe's flat reply. He extended his arm and centered the barrel of the chrome nine-millimeter on Mike's nose.

"Dude, what the hell?" Conner jumped a bit when the gun appeared.

"Where did you get that?" Dave asked.

Joe flicked his eyes to Dave, "Over by the truck tire. The guy must have flung it when he fell or something."

Manny jogged over and put an arm around Joy's shoulders.

Ω

Sirens wailed, as two squad cars shot past their van on their way to answer a call about shots fired at the Oak Brooks Apartment complex. They all rode in stunned silence. Joe finally broke it, "What should I do with this?" He looked down at the gun in his lap.

Manny looked over and shook his head, "I don't know man."

"Just… put it away." Conner put his head in his hands and tried to fight the panic that was ravaging his body. Joy sat next to Dave in the passenger seat and rubbed her head, "Can you believe that son-of-a…"

"Shut your filthy lying mouth." Dave growled through clenched teeth. He kept his eyes fixed on the road while he slowly tried to strangle the steering wheel. "We should have left you back there."

"I swear I didn't know, he…"

Dave chopped her sentence in half, "Save it. You used us. You junkie bitch. You used me and my friends to try to steal for you." Short bursts of air fired out of his nostrils like a bull does as it waits for the right moment to charge the Matador. He looked in the rear-view, "Con, I am so sorry."

Conner inched his eyes up to meet Dave's in the mirror, "I shouldn't be here." Joe and Manny looked over at the sound of Conner's voice. "How does he miss? How does he…" A shudder ran though Conner's body mid-sentence making his teeth click. "There is no way he misses. No way."

Dave spoke first, "I don't have an answer buddy. All I can say is," he looked over at Manny, "Is that I love you. Seriously dude, you saved my life and I man-love you." He looked back at Conner, "He missed me too. I guess he was just a really bad shot."

Conner shrugged and ran a hand through his hair, "Okay… but when I was standing there. I could have reached out and touched the gun, it was that close. A blind fingerless monkey could have hit something four-feet away but this guy just… misses?"

Joe put a hand on Conner's arm, "He just missed dude. You got lucky."

Ω

Conner sat in silence the rest of the way home. The scenario played over in his head dozens of times. The angle of the gun. How close he was. He remembered the muzzle flash and feeling the heat of the blast on his face. The tangy smell of gunpowder and then the pain of hitting his head.

His chest was the proverbial broad side of a barn. What he didn't say out loud in the van, was what he noticed after Dave had helped him up. He didn't say it because he didn't really believe or understand what he saw, and he didn't want to have to try to explain his particular brand of crazy.

He remembered lights and sounds. The back of his head hurt. The sound of another piercing gunshot brought him around and he opened his eyes. He heard Dave talking off to his left. Dave said something about the shooter missing and he knee-jerkingly replied about him being a terrible shot. Shock had taken away the fear.

When Dave grabbed him by the arm and pulled him up he almost lost it; tunnel vision swam in and he heard buzzing but it cleared. There was no blood. No hole into his lung or heart. He checked.

What made his world tilt on it's axis and go fuzzy for a moment was the golf ball sized hole that had ripped an angled swath of asphalt out of the parking space he had been lying in. It was right about where his head had been, he could see the blood on the ground from where he'd hit it when he fell. The shooter was taller than he was, and Conner remembered the gun pointing right at his chest; that image was burned into his memory forever.

He was no geometry major but according to the placement and angle of that hole, that bullet should have passed right through his sternum, maybe missed his heart and blew his right lung out of his back like a New Years Eve party popper filled with pink mist instead of paper streamers. There was no logical way he was sitting in that van.

Ω

Dave's front tire screamed as he ground it into the curb when he parked. Five heads rocked forward then snapped back. Dave threw the gear-shift into park and went back to strangling the steering wheel.

For a brief moment nobody moved, Joe's eyes flicked back and forth from Joy's face to the back of Dave's head. Conner's ears rung in the silence.

"Get out," Dave flatly commanded as he hit the switch to unlock the doors.

"Baby. What's wrong? I swear I didn't know, I…" Dave held up an open palm and Joy clapped her mouth shut.

"I want you to open the door, step out of my van, get into your piece of crap Accord, and drive it off of a cliff." Joe, Conner and Manny all looked at each other with their mouths hung open in *O's* of prideful disbelief. Joy sat for a moment as if considering her next move, when Dave slowly reached across her body and opened the door for her. "Now."

She shook her head and started off toward her car. Joy could feel the four sets of eyes on the back of her skull as she walked and she wanted nothing more than to be out of their judging gaze. With her lips pursed together forming a thin white line of defiance above her chin, Joy unlocked her car, got in and drove out of their lives forever.

Joe broke the silence; with an arm around Conner's neck he leaned forward so he could see the side of Dave's face, "Sooo… what do you guys want to do tonight?"

Ω

As afternoon blurred into evening, the fear and danger slowly faded away, like a vibrant firework blast dissolves into the night. What the four friends were left with was an amazing story of bravery, excitement and heroism which the girls of the Delta Lambda Gamma sorority found very intriguing. Very… intriguing... indeed.

After the revelry ended Conner made his way home and found himself lying in bed, staring blankly at the ceiling. This must be what soldiers go through when they narrowly escape death. PTSD… Shell-Shock… he didn't' know. It all seemed so long ago, and the thing that was driving him crazy was he couldn't make himself feel anything about it. He was numb. When he replayed the event over in his head, it was like he was watching a movie of it.

He was home safe in his bed. The same place he had been this morning, and the poor guy he kept thinking about who got shot at that afternoon in an apartment complex parking lot, was a no-named actor in a B-Movie.

His hand kept absently finding its way up to his chest to check for holes, and for the hundredth time it came up empty. So there he lay; one arm behind his head, the other on an exploratory mission looking for any artificially engineered entrances to his body that had recently been added.

The ceiling was an off-white. It was also covered with that fluffy spackle. When he was a kid someone told him that it was dried cottage cheese. He wasn't a contractor by trade but he was pretty sure that it wasn't dairy. Sleep was tugging at the back of his mind like a child trying to get their father's attention but Conner kept slapping it away.

What if? How? Why? Over and over Conner questioned the empty room and again it stubbornly refused to answer.

Ω

He jerked his head and snapped open his eyes. How long had he been asleep? He craned his neck to see his alarm clock and it told him to relax, it had only been twenty minutes. He still had four hours until he had to get up. With both palms he rubbed his eyes hard. Flashes danced on the back of his eyelids like a strobe light. He had class in the morning and had to get some sleep.

As his vision began to blur he started to see shapes in the cottage cheese. It was a room-sized Rorschach test. A duck, a boat, a face, a clown (as an aside, he hated clowns so he quickly moved on to the next shape). The soft yellow light of the desk lamp on his nightstand cast a sideways shadow across the room and gave the shapes on the ceiling a real depth; a 3-D quality.

When patterns occur in nature it draws the eye. Nature is random, wild and unpredictable. When submerged ocean stones seem to line up in uniformed tidiness, divers think they've found Atlantis. It's human nature to look for meaning and purpose in what seems like happenstance. That fascination holds true when any unexpected pattern appears where it shouldn't. As Conner drifted off to sleep a line in the ceiling caught his eye.

Odd, he hadn't noticed it before. It looked like it ran from about where his nightstand was to the closet door; eight feet away. Maybe it was a sagging two-by-four pushing through the sheet-rock. He blinked and it was more pronounced. The shadow had grown and some of the cottage cheese had snowed down on his carpet by the door.

Plumbing. The upstairs neighbor's toilet must be flooding and his room was about to be transformed into a Wild Rivers water-park ride. As he was about to sit up to line his carpet with towels he noticed a second beam; this one even bigger than the first. It dropped down out of the ceiling a few feet from the foot of his bed.

A few things alarmed him about his current situation. The first was the speed at which the support structures keeping an entire floor of an apartment building off of his head were failing. Second, and even more immediate and disturbing than his potential death by crushing, was the fact that he couldn't move.

Conner tried to sit up, but it felt like an invisible elephant had used him as a beanbag chair. He fought to pull his arm up from his side and all he managed was a sad wiggle of his index finger. Fear dove into his eyes, sprinted through his brain and made it's way to his toes. He tried to scream to Dave but found his throat was suffering the same malady as the rest of his body.

Rational thought was slowly packing up shop and getting ready to leave. Every logical explanation for what was happening to him was slowly being eliminated. Bells-Palsy, Stroke, Schizophrenia?

A splintering crunch snapped Conner's attention back to the ceiling. The two beams had sunk down at least a foot and were breaking through the dry-wall and spackle. Conner's eyes were wide and frantic. Then one beam, the one furthest from him started to move.

That is when Conner truly broke with reality.

"I'm insane. There it is. I'm one of those people who will shortly be pushing a shopping cart I stole from Wal-Mart, full of empty cat-food cans, and having in-depth discussions on the current political state-of-affairs on Mars with a mailbox," he thought.

The beam crashed through the molding of the recessed lighting in the bathroom sending glass and debris raining down to the floor. Adrenaline felt like it was going to start pumping out of his ears with each heartbeat. The second beam seemed to almost roll toward him as well. How was no one else hearing this? Was Dave asleep? Maybe he'd already been crushed to death.

The first beam pivoted when it was six or so feet from him and landed directly over him, head-to-toe parallel. The second beam then decided to defy gravity. And why wouldn't it? At this point Conner was almost so far gone that he began to happily accept the incredible. The second beam flipped, and landed over the first. An unmistakable shape now sat magically suspended over Conner's paralyzed body.

A cross. A ten foot, wooden cross filled Conner's vision. He whispered a silent prayer that didn't make much sense but at the moment they were the only two words he could put together, "Please God. Please God. Please God..."

That's when it started. It started off as a whisper and grew in volume like an approaching train.

It hijacked his thoughts and thumped its way into his consciousness like a bass drum. It was a voice that he couldn't quite put a finger on. Deep and light at the same time. Full of authority and passion one moment, soft and nurturing the next. It was foreign, but much like every other thing in this paradox, in a way he couldn't explain or understand he had heard this voice all of his life.

It resonated within his head. Bounced off the walls of his mind. As he lay there, reality tried to kick the door in and offered up something more immediate and concrete to worry about. *What if some of the cottage-cheese spackle drops into my eye? I won't be able to wipe it away. I could go blind.*

That was when the whisper turned the dial up to ten. A single word repeated. Simple yet complex; a plea and a command. It drowned out all of the other neurotic babble mumbling away in Conner's brain.

"*Believe.*"

It was as if a metaphorical fist punched him in his very real stomach. The wind rushed out of his lungs but when he drew in a new breath something unexpected came with it.

Peace.

It was a peace he had felt earlier that day. Right before the firing pin struck the small blasting cap that ignited the gunpowder, which sent the nine-millimeter slug rocketing at his chest at thirteen-hundred feet per second. At that moment a sense of calm poured over him like warm honey. It just slowly filled him up. As Conner lay frozen on his bed and inhaled, he felt it again, like an old friend stopping by for a visit.

It was warm. Soft. Comforting. It felt like home. It settled over him like the wool blanket his mother used to tuck him in each night before bed when he was small.

Conner silently mouthed the word; a tear ran down the side of his face and dove into his pillow. He was aware of sensations. The rhythmic sound of his own shallow breathing; the feel of the down comforter bunched beneath the small of his back; the warmth that was flushing his cheeks.

Then he saw it. It just appeared. One second nothing... the next, light. From the middle of the cross a tiny dot of light appeared. It was bright... pure; like no other light he'd ever seen. He wanted to squint but found that his eyelids had joined the growing list of body-parts on strike. Then it began to grow, and as it grew, it grew in intensity.

It was as if the dirty paper bag he lived in was being ripped open from above and the light from another universe was flooding in for the first time.

Tears now flowed freely from the corners of his eyes soaking a small oasis into the pillow case on either side of his head.

"*Believe... Believe...*" The voice became more clear and crisp with every pronunciation. The light was beautiful and blinding. It was like the sun; a million suns all rolled into one. It made him feel very small, but that was alright because he felt safe. Everything vanished into white. He thought he'd gone blind. That was when someone cleared their throat next to him. Maybe three feet or so from his left ear... someone-cleared-their-throat. Someone was in the room with him.

Just as the disaster center of his brain was about to hit the self-destruct button and go nuclear, a hand settled gently on his left shoulder. It was a hand. A real hand. When the fingers on that hand pressed into the flesh of his chest, the world went away. Warm electricity pulsed through his body making him hold his breath. The power was incredible.

That hand could create worlds and destroy universes. He didn't know how he knew that but he just did. There was a long pause. Conner could hear the fabric of their clothing rustle and rub as they inched closer to his bed. They must have been kneeling next to him because he could feel proximity; hot breath on his neck.

Then the same voice spoke, but this time it wasn't a thought in his head, it was a man's voice talking directly into his left ear.

"*Conner. I have always been with you. You've never been alone.*"

Emotion welled up in his soul. Sobs racked his frozen body.

The voice continued, "*I will always be with you my son. I just ask that you trust me. Believe in me.*"

Conner couldn't speak so he simply thought back, "Can it be you? You're here? You don't exist. Why? I don't deserve for you to be here." Shame dumped over him like mud. He wanted to hide.

The hand pressed firmly down into Conner's chest. It was rough and calloused and strong. "*You don't deserve my mercy son; I love you because I love you. Look to the cross. Believe. I will never leave you.*" If it was possible the light intensified.

Ω

"I do!" Conner screamed into the empty room. He shot up in bed and looked to his left. Tears still clung to his face. He sat for a moment propped up with his arms locked behind him, chest heaving trying to catch his breath.

It took a few seconds for his brain to catch up with his eyes. The desk lamp was still spilling its soft yellow light across the room. The only sounds were that of the sprinkler outside his window watering the sidewalk, and his own heavy breathing. The ceiling was back to normal. No noise, no critical structural damage to the load-bearing support beams above his head, and no one he could see in his room.

Oh… and he could move. That fact hit him like a truck, and he leapt to his feet to prove it to himself. He danced in a circle as if he were trying to shake off a colony of ants that had nested in his shirt.

"Dream. Dream?" he questioned the clock and it told him it was five-thirty in the morning. As the seconds passed the vivid details began to fade. The emotion was replaced with disbelief and his rational brain began offering suggestions. Maybe it was something he ate? He had heard that eating late could cause the mind to go on some strange late-night adventures.

He tousled his hair in exasperation and sat down on the edge of the bed; elbows on knees, head in hands. It had been a crazy day. Neurotic worry got his attention by nibbling at the corner of his mind. When he reached for his alarm clock to make sure it was set, his hand hit a book on his night stand. The book fluttered to the floor and landed spine down, pages open.

He stared at it for a few moments. It was his brown leather-bound bible. The one his grandmother had given him for his birthday when he was twelve. The one he had shoved to the very back of his dresser drawer and that hadn't seen the light of day for over a year. Conner was positive that he hadn't taken it out of solitary confinement. How did it end up on his nightstand? The world tilted on it's axis for a tick and visions of Conner's dream somersaulted through his mind.

When his hand came within a few inches he paused. Fears of being shocked, or it being some kind of a trap ran through his mind, but he quickly dismissed them. When the tip of his index finger touched the fine tissue-paper like pages of the book he heard a voice in his head.

"Believe."

The word hit him like a fist to the stomach. Conner pulled his hand back like he had stuck it on the red-hot burner of a stove-top.

"Okay this is stupid," he said aloud to reassure himself. "It's a book," he reached down and grabbed it with a purpose; like he was trying to show it who's boss. "A creepy ghost bible that can apparently move on it's own, but a book none-the-same."

The book sat on his lap, and it fell open to a random page. It was a dry raspy sound. The Second Book of Samuel.

"The Lord is my rock, my fortress and my deliverer." He liked the way that sounded. It was manly. With a finger he scanned up to see that he was reading Second Samuel, verse twenty-two. It was called David's song of praise. He kept reading, *"My God is my rock, in whom I take refuge, my shield and the horn of my salvation. He is my stronghold, my refuge and my savior – from violent men you save me."*

He stopped reading and stared blankly at the floor. From violent men you save me. With a blink he was back in that parking lot. Gravel crunching under his shoe as he pivoted on the ball of his foot. The smell of the breeze and the sun making him squint as it gleamed off of the end that nine millimeter. He saw the muzzle pop like a paparazzi flash bulb over and over again. The scene replayed and he kept coming to the same unbelievable conclusion.

A chill ran up his spine as he mentally disproved his morbid hypothesis. He should be dead. Dead. His story should have reached it's tragic final page next to that lifted truck in that stupid apartment complex parking lot, but it didn't. A burning sensation in his chest reminded him that he was holding his breath and he exhaled.

Conner pressed his brow with a combination of confusion and curiosity. With a few awkward movements he was positioned on his bed with two pillows underneath his shoulders and his head propped up on the wall behind him. He skimmed for a few minutes but with a quick flip of his thumb he saw that he book was close to a hundred pages long and he was having trouble seeing now because he was so tired.

"Tomorrow," he promised he the bible. Conner waited a second for a response but the book was being shy. "Tomorrow then." The pillow had barley touched the back of his head before he drifted off. Through a groggy lazy fog he tried to mutter a short incoherent prayer before sleep took him. He failed.

Ω

MEEP, MEEP, MEEP! Conner's eyes shot open like a set of spring loaded window blinds. He lay there and waited for his brain to boot up. It was much too light in his room for what time it should have been. As he wiped a chunk of sleep from his eye he looked at his alarm clock and saw it was eight-thirteen. That gave him about five minutes to get ready and seven minutes to get to class.

Ω

The dull gray light from the top of his bathroom mirror shone down on him making him look sick and gaunt. He hated the way he looked in that mirror. He stood there with his arms locked on the countertop and leaned forward to study his face. There was a cut on his right temple that must have happened yesterday when he fell. The scab crumbled off in tiny flakes as he rubbed it. The back of his head was killing him. He winced as he explored the Goose-Egg with a finger.

He flipped through the Cliff-Notes of yesterday in his mind. It all seemed so long ago. Then there was that dream. That dream was surreal. Amazing. He looked at the Bible lying face-down on his comforter and his eyes softened. He'd have to remember to read the rest of that chapter he started when he got home today.

The sleep-timer ran out and his alarm clock started to yell at him again. A wall shaking "Thud" from next door was

Dave's way of asking Conner to turn it off. He snapped back to the present. There was no way he was going to be on time to class.

As he ran out the door the sly voice of reason began to whisper to him. It rattled off a myriad of other things and worries he had in his life to deal with at the moment. Too many to take precious time to read a two-thousand year old book. That book will always be there if you need it. But it's just not at the top of our list.

Ω

Time passed as it always does in life and Conner became swept up in the everyday grind of his routine. He never got around to reading that section of the Bible he was curious about. After being on his nightstand for about a week it found it's way to the corner of his bathroom counter, then to the third shelf of his bookcase.

He actually held it for a few seconds when he used it to turn a Black Widow spider that had been haunting his dreams into a grease spot on the wall. Eventually the Bible found it's way to the back of a drawer, and the very back of Conner's mind.

The events of that cold spring day never truly left Conner, he just always found himself thinking that he had all the time in the world to go back and read; or study; or pray. Right now, at this very moment he was having too much fun drinking, and having too much trouble passing his classes to fill his life with another whole relationship. Especially with God. There would be time.

V. Nicholas Gerasimou

CHAPTER 2

THE JOY OF JOY: BEHIND THE VEIL

THE JOY OF JOY:
BEHIND THE VEIL

Sariel stood behind his charge. Over the eons he had been assigned to watch over countless numbers of The Lord's children. He had fought in, and waged epic battles in the heavens, been The Lord's hand in momentous moments in human history and sat in the full glory of The Most High.

Today he stood behind a young man in a dirty apartment living room. The Lord had told him that this particular young man had an important role to play in spreading His word to the world. The "when" and "where" of Conner's message were kept a mystery to Sariel. He was simply instructed to stand watch over him and prevent the Evil One from having access. So Sariel stood.

Appearance, in angelic terms was a very fluid concept. They existed in a realm outside of the four-dimensional box humans were caged in until they were set free. Appearance changed with need and mood. They were all created by The Most High in perfection, but the fall had darkened some.

Angels, as God's children had come to call them, were meant to be beautiful messengers of light. The legions who fell with his brother Lucifer during the rebellion, were twisted with their hatred.

Darkness and loathing had contorted their minds which

in turn had changed their physical forms into grotesque perversions of The Lord's perfection. They were the monsters and demons that had haunted the dreams of mankind for time immemorial. Dark venomous creatures that scarcely resembled the glorious holy messengers Jesus had thought into existence at the beginning.

At the moment, in a physical human sense, Sariel was a creature to behold. He was standing in a plane which was unnoticeable to Conner. This was by design. Throughout history when he or his kind had been commanded to appear to the humans, the terror they were met with was almost palpable. Even in their most tame and timid forms, angels were mighty and intimidating beings.

The crown of Sariel's head nearly touched the vaulted ceiling of the living room. A gleaming white calf-length tunic draped over his muscular body and was cinched together at the waist with a plain rope belt. Over one shoulder, a scabbard was slung with a sword that literally hummed with holy power. From hilt to tip, the weapon was taller than Conner was standing on the tips of his toes, but it fit well into Sariel's bear-paw sized hands. He ran a hand through his shoulder length brown hair as the other young man walked past him toward the couch.

Conner's friend David sat down next to him and the two began to banter. It seemed they were planning on a day of drunkenness and debauchery. He shook his head and looked at Conner. How could God's children do anything but worship Him? They had received the most precious gift possible but yet they continued to rebel. He had to remind himself that it was The Lord's will for them to be tested and to come to Him of their own free will.

Ω

When the car carrying Joy screeched to a halt outside of the apartment, Sariel immediately felt their presence. With a thought he was outside on the lawn, sword in hand. Joy and David embraced by the curb while they crawled off the hood. He knew them all by name; at least by the names they had back when they were all brothers in the kingdom.

Three of them; their dark, leathered scaly skin swam beneath a garment that looked to be a patchwork of constantly moving raw animal hides held together with black twine. They unlatched curved razor sharp talons from the hood and roof of the car and stood defiantly behind Joy.

Sariel's back was four feet across. He rolled his neck and flexed his arms. David and Joy walked up the lawn toward the front door and her three escorts followed. With an explosion of power, Sariel snapped open the impossibly white wings that grew out of the coiled muscles of his back, and stretched them to span. Tip to tip they essentially covered the entire front entrance of the apartment blocking any view.

The three flinched and stopped their advance. They looked at each other and back to the white guardian. The larger of the three stepped forward and held out his hands, talons up.

"Hello Sariel."

"Munkar. Why are you here?"

Munkar drummed his fingers on a rusted, crooked sword hanging from his waist, "We are simply going where we are permitted. No more… no less," he looked Sariel up and down like a man examining a used car he doesn't quite trust, "You look well."

Sariel spun his sword and sunk it tip down into the ground in front of him, "I wish I could say the same."

A sly smile slowly spread across Munkar's face like an approaching storm front, revealing rows of gnarled jagged teeth, "Our little one has quite a day planned for your little sheep. It should be interesting to watch."

Sariel leaned forward on his sword, "You," He waved a finger back and forth into each of their distorted pig-like faces, "Are not permitted to touch him."

Munkar looked back at his two compatriots and they each exchanged a smirk, "We won't need to. Not with what we have planned."

"Nothing you do can alter what the Most High wills," Sariel replied.

"We'll see brother." Munkar turned and the three demons walked back to the car and stood patiently like sentinels by the passenger side door.

With one forceful yank Sariel pulled his sword from the ground and slid it into the scabbard on his back, "Yes, we shall see."

Ω

When Conner's group left the house on their way to meet Joy's ex-partner, three of Sariel's brethren arrived. Ambriel, Gagiel and Remiel rocketed out of the heavens like shooting stars, and landed next to Sariel on the front lawn. They were glorious beings, shining with light as Sariel was. Massive and beautiful as the Lord had created them.

As the five drove away in David's dilapidated green van, Ambriel placed a hand on Sariel's shoulder.

"We will prevail. The Lord wills it."

Sariel nodded and clasped the hand, "Praise be to God."

"Praise be to God!" The three echoed. Then in the blink of an eye the four angelic beings vanished.

Ω

They looked like crows. Evil demonic crows. They filled the trees, lined the rooftops and defiantly lurked around the apartment grounds. Sariel and his three brethren stood below the staircase that lead to Mike's apartment. The demons had essentially filled the walkway at the entrance to the landing, where Conner and his group were conversing with the one called Mike.

Sariel turned to Ambriel, "Keep watch and ensure that they have an escape path from the landing when things turn."

Ambriel nodded and walked over to the base of the stairs. He drew his sword and stood facing the seven dark creatures that eyed him with hate. From up above the shouting escalated and then David began pounding on the door. Excitement ricocheted through the throngs of fallen angels. They chattered and clicked like a swarm of cicadas filling the Southern nighttime sky. Sariel leapt up to the landing and stood on the railing behind Manny, Joseph and Conner.

Joy's companions stood three abreast on the roof above the front door. Munkar held out his arms in a welcoming gesture and smiled, "It seems things are about to get interesting brother."

Sariel drew his sword, "Praise Be To The Lamb! Praise Be To The Holy Lion Jesus!" Gagiel and Remiel echoed Sariel's prayer from below and slowly drew their swords. Then there was a moment of pause. The build-up had ended. The rollercoaster like sense of anticipation was poised at the precipice and was ready to drop off that first gut-wrenching cliff into madness.

Munkar looked dead into Sariel's eyes, "We shall see." Joy's foot met Mike's crotch and she bolted down the stairs. Demons vaulted into the air like dust and descended onto the group of four. Ambriel charged the group at the base of the stairs like a bull and carved a way out for Conner and the others just as they reached the last step. From above, Sariel corkscrewed into the air and began to hack and slash a path of light above his charge.

The clangs and crashes of angelic steel meeting, and the screeches of the fallen as the holy blades of the four protectors dismembered and snuffed out their abysmal existence rose to a deafening pitch.

Gagiel and Ramiel stood on the path which the four friends were running toward the parking lot on, like bookends. In front of them were dozens of evil roadblocks. Swords drawn and profanity flowing, they waited for the four humans like sharks in murky water. The two looked at each other, "God wills it!" Gagiel yelled. Ramiel nodded and the two surged forward and began to cut a path. They danced around each other in a ballet of carnage. They spoke to each other in angelic tongues that would have been lost on human ears as they dodged and slashed; parried and pierced. It was a choreographed routine they had perfected over the eons. It was very effective.

Conner, Manny and Dave fanned out in front of the truck. Joe stayed behind to fend off the stragglers. Ambriel stood behind him, sword in hand like a massive muscled shadow. Joe swung his bat in an arc in front of him as Ambriel's sword swung over his head like a helicopter blade severing two attackers at the waist and splashing unseen gallons of black blood down around the humans.

Sariel looked down from a vantage point dozens of feet above Conner's head. He was covered in gore and his own set of wounds, but the Lord sustained him. His companions were occupied, fending off the ranks of the fallen. There seemed to be an unending supply.

Below him Conner has stopped near the front of the truck and David had grabbed hold of the girl. The one called Mike was screaming at the girl, and Munkar had climbed onto the back of the twisted young man standing to Mike's left. Sariel could see that the light of God was not in the heart of the young man. He was one of the lost. Munkar's voice must have almost sounded like his own.

Conner stepped forward and Munkar screamed into the young man's ear to stop him. The gun appeared and drew a line on Conner's heart. In the frozen moments that followed Munkar looked up and found Sariel in the chaos and smiled a sick, victorious smile. He opened his arms and leapt off of Killian's back into the air toward where Sariel was hovering.

Killian's finger added the extra pound of pressure on the trigger and the firing pin hit the blasting cap on the bullet. The powder ignited and the expanding gasses forced the slug out of the barrel of the gun with flame and a flash of light.

Sariel rocketed down at an impossible speed and landed in between his charge and the small chunk of flying metal.

Munkar's scream ripped his attention skyward again. The demon's face was twisted with rage and his sword was held high over head ready to deliver a finishing blow to Conner's protector.

Bullet and foe in air, Sariel closed his eyes and called out to the Lord. He opened them in time to see the tip of Gagiel's sword open a causeway into Munkar's ribcage. The rest of the sword followed suit with Gagiel close behind. He hit Munkar mid-air like a run-away truck blasting through a busy intersection. The two tumbled off beyond the sidewalk into some shrubbery.

His attention snapped back to the subsonic piece of lead. The bullet was feet from Conner's chest. Sariel could feel the air displacement radiating away from it as it flew. He called out to the Lord to give him permission to intercede on His behalf.

His eyes shot open again, "Thank you Lord!" Sariel spun and faced Conner. He looked so frail. All humans did. So small and weak in this world. They had no idea what the Lord was willing to give them in the next. He shook the thought away and made his move. The bullet was inches from ending Conner's time on Earth.

Sariel reached out and put both his hands through the middle of Conner's torso. Time and space bent around his clasped fingers and for a single moment Conner was transparent. If only the man Einstein had known how close he really was to understanding a simple truth about the reality The Lord had created.

The bullet hummed through the hole and shattered on the asphalt leaving a small hole. Conner fell backwards hitting his head but otherwise he was unharmed.

$$\Omega$$

Later that night Sariel stood over Conner's bed while he slept. He loved Conner because the Lord loved Conner. Over the eons he had been entrusted to protect countless numbers of the Lord's children and he felt honored and blessed each and every time. Jesus had a plan for this young man and Sariel would be a tool in letting him achieve it.

It was now his job to give this young man a vision. To plant a seed in a dream that would germinate much later and produce fruit.

The instrument of The Lord's torture that the humans had adopted to represent his sacrifice; the cross. An image of the cross would certainly get Conner's attention. Real; visceral; loud. A little fear wouldn't hurt either. Sariel always had a little flare for the dramatic and he thought the threat of the building collapsing would get the desired affect.

As spackle and drywall sifted down on the boy, emotion flowed out of him. Then the unexpected. Immediately Sariel dropped to both knees. Power and light filled the room. The Creator had come to speak to the boy. This was exciting.

Jesus knelt next to the boy and whispered into his ear. He placed a hand on his shoulder and reassured him. How blessed this child was. Sariel looked at the ground and smiled. How blessed.

Ω

Sariel watched with sadness as the bright vibrant emotions from that day wore off of Conner like how the smell of a new car is slowly replaced by the musty aroma of gym socks. He watched as Conner sinned. He watched Conner put The Lord in the backseat of his mind and dive head-long into the alluring call of college life.

Nights of drunkenness and debauchery were followed by days of sloth. Sariel stood behind the boy on nights of sin and lust and lamented the young man's weakness. Meaningless flesh filled encounters with nameless women dotted his calendar. Hours spent on the computer searching for images. Traveling to websites that were hand-made by the will of the evil-one. The seductive videos of carnal fantasies Conner looked at on the computer slowly made dents in, and finally began to take little chips out of his soul. Profanity and anger flowed out of the mouth that should have been proclaiming the glory of God. Conner slowly slipped back into selfish darkness. Humans were a mystery to the angel. He shook his head and prayed for the boy.

The Lord was called on in moments of nostalgia or fear, but the relationship was a long distance one. Time passed and Sariel kept watch. A silent protector of a spoiled, disobedient, prodigal child.

The only saving grace was the end of the school year. Summer meant Conner would travel home to be with his family. Home and away from this sinful environment. That thought brought his guardian some peace. His family had a calming effect on him that Sariel enjoyed. It would not be June soon enough.

CHAPTER 3

THE FIVE TIME:

V. Nicholas Gerasimou

THE FIVE TIME

Conner jabbed his finger on each date on the calendar as he counted. "Three days until we go little buddy." He closed the kitchen cabinet door that the calendar depicting Labrador Retrievers, in various hi-lar-i-ous positions wearing human clothing was taped to.

"I know, I'm pretty fired up. *Finally* twenty-one." Came Steven's reply from the couch. Conner's little brother lay feet crossed on the Love-Seat watching television. "Vegas…" he opened his arms and seemed to savor the word like one does a sip of fine wine.

Conner smiled and opened the refrigerator. He peered in and stared blankly at the sparse pickings. His parents needed to go shopping. A Costco run perhaps? He pulled his head out and craned his neck toward the living room, "So we're good for Friday night before we leave right?"

Steven popped his head up like a Prairie Dog, "We're leaving Saturday morning on the bright right?"

"Yeah… but I told you that Adrian wanted us to go to that church service on Friday night at that church he youth pastors at," Conner mumbled as he shoved his back into the barren ice-box.

Steven sat up, "I don't want to go to some hand-holding feel good sing-a-thon. Come on dude. Your buddy Adrian is a cool guy, but he's a little…"

Conner leaned on the fridge door, "What?"

"I don't know," Steven looked up as he searched for the word as if it were etched on the ceiling, "Magoo."

"Magoo?"

"Yeah… Magoo. He's a little too nice, and just kind of…" Steven shrugged, "Magoo."

Conner closed the fridge and walked over to the couch, "Come on man, I kind of promised him we'd go."

"You promised without asking me?" Steven asked.

Conner smiled and smacked his lips, "Look, it wouldn't kill you to go to church. It's like a youth group thing. Lots of young college-y type people. It'll be alright."

Steven flicked his big-brother in the shoulder making him flinch, "When's the last time you went to church anyway?"

"Two weeks ago," Came Conner's defensive reply.

"That doesn't count. You went because of that hot girl you showed me on Facebook. You went to high-school with her and she asked you to go," he put his hands over his heart and fluttered his eyes, "Oh Conner, you're so noble. Praise be to the God… in your pants."

Shame washed over Conner's face and his cheeks flushed. He was a bit annoyed that his little brother had so effortlessly dismantled his ruse and exposed him as the hypocrite he was. That made him angry. He had to quickly reestablish dominance in this sibling paradigm, so he did the only thing he could think of to restore order to the world. He used violence.

"Oww, dude!" Steven fell backward as Conner's fist met him square in the chest. "What the hell?"

Conner, satisfied that the hierarchy of the household was intact continued making his case, "Look, I went to church because I wanted to go and it's good to go. The girl was just a… happy coincidence."

Steven pulled himself up and straightened out his shirt, "Okay…" he said dripping with sarcasm.

"Besides, there'll be food there," he added.

Steven nodded, "I'm listening."

"And hundreds of college girls looking for a good Christian man to sweep them off their feet," Conner continued to sweeten the pot.

Steven crossed his arms over his chest and thoughtfully put his chin in his hand, "Proceed sir."

Now for the kill shot, "Plus, we'll have to go to church to pray for some forgiveness for all of the disgusting... and awesome things we are about to partake in this weekend. Think about it."

A few moments passed and Steven remained immovably stoic. He then reached out with slow deliberation and placed his extended index finger in the middle of his big brother's forehead and left it there for a few uncomfortable moments. Conner crossed his eyes and furrowed his brow to look at it.

"Sold."

"Yes!" Conner jumped and clapped in triumph. "So we'll go on Friday night, be home around ten or so, get some sleep, and head on out."

"All the guys know what time to be here right?"

Conner nodded, "Yup. They're big boys. They have watches."

"Who's coming for sure?"

Conner counted on his fingers, "Rich, Brian and Gabe."

"Cool."

Conner grabbed his little brother by the cheeks and smashed them together, "It'll be an epic weekend little Stevie."

"Don't call me Stevie," but with his face held together it came out more like, "Don'ch kallah meh Schteeviee." Conner smiled. He loved this kid.

Ω

What transpired from three-thirty-seven to four-twelve p.m. could only later be recalled in panicked, fear-filled snapshots. They all added small details and extra layers of substance to help flesh the story out. It was hard to understand what really happened. When the friends spoke of it, the events were discussed in hushed, head-shaking, disbelieving tones. Everything was jumbled and disjointed. It took them weeks to sort it out.

The five had a hell of a time.

Ω

This couldn't be happening. This had to be a dream, or a hallucination. Conner's panic stricken mind was stuck on repeat. It was all he could mutter to himself as he fell to his knees. A shard of broken beer bottle poked through his jeans and sliced his leg as he reached for Brian's arm. He barely noticed.

"Wha... what happened?" Brian asked. His words came out in slow thick chunks, like his tongue was covered in glue.

"Get over here! Hurry!" Conner kept his back to the wall and pulled Brian to him keeping the chaos of the room in his field of vision. Brian moaned as he was forced to move but the plate that exploded near his head seemed to motivate him more than Conner's coaxing could. With a few quick kicks of his legs he was pressed up against the wall taking in the carnage that continued to erupt around them.

"Seriously," he put a hand to the back of his head and winced, "What the hell happened?"

"You got hit."

"With what?" He reached back again and this time his fingers came back from their exploratory journey covered with blood. Slowly the fog that had been clouding his thoughts cleared enough for him to start connecting some dots. "Where is everybody?"

"I don't know!" Conner snapped back. He frantically scanned the crowd in front of him for Steven. His chest began to tighten at the thought of his baby brother somewhere in the middle of this.

Brian pulled himself up to a crouch next to his friend.

"We gotta get outta here. I'll go…"

Brian's voice trailed off into empty space. Through the mass of bodies, Conner caught a glimpse of Steven, fighting valiantly but outnumbered. Places in Conner's brain that had never been accessed before powered up and sprung to life. The places where fear… true fear were kept. Places where we all store hate and rage and death. It's where panic grows into desperation, and desperation explodes into blind fury.

Adrenaline coursed into Conner's veins; he drew in one long ragged breath as he rose to his feet. Steven landed a two fisted shot to the side of someone's face that happened to be in front of him. The man spat blood on the floor like a tobacco chewer aiming for a spittoon. Steven was frantic and swinging at anything that moved. He drew his arm back and his elbow connected to a random neck behind him drawing the attention of a large hulk-of-a-man who was previously occupied elsewhere.

Conner saw all of it in slow motion. Every detail burned into his eyes like the outline of the sun when stared at too long. "Stevie!"

As Steven looked up expectantly at the sound of his brother's voice, an elbow came crashing down on the back of his neck sending him to his knees with a wince. Conner's eyes widened. The hulk whom Steven had elbowed threw a knee into his ribs dropping him to his hip. As he gathered himself again and turned to face his attacker, the man drew back his leg and slammed the tip of his black steel-toed work boot behind Steven's left ear, like he was trying to start a motorcycle.

All of the air sucked out the room. There was no sound; no heat; no cold… there was nothing. The world ripped by around him at breakneck speed, but Conner couldn't see it. Conner watched Steven fall to the floor. That's all he saw. The look of pain slipped off of his face as he lost consciousness like a satin sheet being slowly pulled off a bed.

He was so small… alone. When Steven's shoulder hit the side of the bar, Conner was already moving. Frantic urgency. All he could see was his baby brother. His loving, sweet, goofy brother. A primal protection instinct hijacked his brain. The most dangerous man in the world is one who loves something more than himself. One who is unflinchingly willing to sacrifice his blood, safety and life if needed to protect the thing that he loves. Conner loved his little brother.

Blood hammered behind his ears like an enraged river about to breach the levy and wipe out a town. Drums echoed inside his head. Deep base drums. Hate, panic, rage and fear shook the bars of his soul. They wanted out. That was all Conner could hear as he ran. All he could feel. The world began to shake. His vision blurred, and then there was darkness.

Ω

The scream was frantic and wild. It took a few moments to realize that it was coming from him. Conner felt hands on his shoulders and he began to come back to himself. The world was a blur of lights, yelling, the musty smell of old cigarette smoke, varnished wood and blood. His chest hurt. It hurt to breathe.

He heard Rich's voice urging him to, "Get the hell up and stop fighting me!" The warm sunlight hit his face, car doors slammed shut, tires burned and they were gone.

Ω

Brian's knee popped as he crouched next to Conner, "We gotta get outta here. I'll go get Rich and Gabe. Maybe the car. Con? Con!" The crowd parted and he caught a glimpse of Steven over near the bar. Conner called his name and then Brian lost line-of-sight again as the crowd shifted. Relief washed over him and he reached over to grab Conner's arm to get his attention when Conner screamed.

It startled him and he jerked his hand back like he'd accidently touched the side of a pot of boiling oil. It was a frantic scream that flirted with crazy. Spittle and tears flew from his face as he called Steven's name. His face flushed a crimson red and every vein stood out on his neck and threatened to burst. Brian sat back in momentary shock. All of Conner's muscles tensed for a moment as if he were loading to jump off the third tier of an Olympic high-dive, and then he was gone.

Brian reached out and used a nearby table to steady himself as he stood. He moved a bit to the left so he could look down the ally Conner had created in the crowd. It was like the Red Sea parting for Moses. His friend was a juggernaut; he bowled through the mob.

A man in a red flannel shirt side-stepped into Conner's path. In a melee, the concepts of right and wrong, friend and foe become blurred. Survival instincts take over and all bodies in proximity become potential targets. Self preservation and advancing your position become the primary priorities.

The man regained his balance and raised his eyes in time to see two-hundred and thirty pounds of hate crash into him. The crown of Conner's head met him just under his chin. He landed several feet away in a twisted heap. Conner never broke stride. He could see his brother in snap-shots through gaps between people's legs and breaks in the crowd. He was a torpedo in the water.

Someone grabbed his arm and in an unconscious fluid movement Conner wrapped his hand around three of the offending digits and wrenched them backwards breaking them at the knuckle. The unfortunate person attached to those fingers recoiled and wailed in pain and Conner took the opportunity to clamp his free hand over the man's Adam's-apple and use him as a battering ram to clear a path to his brother.

An errant fist caught him in the temple, an elbow slammed into his ribs; nothing slowed Conner's powerful jogging gate. From Brian's point of view it was a sight to see. In a strange way, that he couldn't quite explain it was almost beautiful. But as beautiful, or poetic or… whatever it was, that was as knife the man to Conner's right had in his hand.

It flashed from the crowd and blood began pouring from a four inch gash that opened up at the bottom of Conner's left collarbone to just above his nipple. Brian screamed, Conner plowed ahead.

In normal situations most sane people have notions of human decency, morality, mercy and the legal repercussions of their actions. Even in moments of extreme stress there is a voice that warns and calms; that sets a limit of what you're willing and able to do. The only voice Conner could hear was his own roar.

The human shield fell limp to the ground when Conner let go to sprint the final few feet. After stepping on the unconscious man's neck, he slid in sideways on his hip and grabbed Steven's shoulders.

"Stevie? Stevie, look at me buddy!"

Steven's eyes fluttered as he tried to focus on his big brother.

"Hey, it's okay. I'm here and we're gonna get outta here. Let's go."

Steven coughed and vomited down the front of his shirt as he began to shake.

"Come on buddy; Hey! Look at me Stevie!" He cradled his brother's head lightly in his hands and wiped away a dot of blood by his eye with his thumb. "Oh my God, oh my God, oh my God…" Conner pulled Steven close and held him as he rocked. The blood pouring from the opening in his chest was warm on his skin as it soaked them both.

A buzz rippled through the crowd and a new energy kindled the dying embers of the brawl back into a roaring fire. Before Conner could stand a crowd surge rushed towards where he and his brother were huddled. He spun to protect his kin. A deep guttural growl began to rattle from somewhere deep inside Conner's chest; more animal than human.

With teeth bared and fists clenched he dove into the sea of bodies kicking, swinging and screaming.

Ω

"Hey," Rich slapped Gabe on the shoulder, "I'm gonna go take a leak."

"Hold up I gotta go too," Gabe said as he got up from the table. He looked at Conner, "Order me another beer, and… some nachos if the waitress ever comes by again."

Conner belched an acknowledgement. Rich and Gabe headed down the dark hallway that led to the bathrooms. The only light came from the occasional red flash of the neon "*Pisser*" sign hanging on the back wall of the corridor, and the dirty yellow glow from under the door. As the two traveled down the ill-lit tunnel (that's what it felt like; not a hallway but a dingy tunnel) a small piece of economic social-commentary acted as the pebble, dropped on the top of a snow covered mountain-side, which would eventually roll into a boulder of calamity and lead to them all fighting for their lives.

Hesperia had fallen on hard times since the housing bubble burst back in 2008. Unemployment was skyrocketing which meant people were spending less. Spending less on things like eating out. Eating out at places like The Rusty Spoke Bar & Grille. With revenue dropping the mom-and-pop establishments which didn't have corporate backing fell first.

They let the little things go. Things that didn't seem like a big deal at the time. A light bulb here, a scratched countertop there. Maybe the linoleum in the bathroom hallway began to roll up at the edges; who has the time or money to fix those kind of things?

"Why are we here?" Gabe asked.

Rich shrugged, "Dude, I don't know. I told Brian that we could have just powered through to Baker and grabbed a Gyro at the Mad Greek, but he *had* to eat."

"This place sucks." Gabe said as he ran a finger along the oily wall in disgust.

Rich gave the hallway a tepid look, "No argument here."

Gabe turned his head, "Well I'm not sure I'd even trust

the food here. You see that wait…" He swallowed the end of his sentence as his foot caught the lip of the worn linoleum. He pitched forward, arms spinning like an animated weather vane in a nor'easter.

"Hey there buddy!" Rich said as he latched on to the back of Gabe's shirt to steady him.

"Thanks."

"Yup. No prob."

"Dude, that would have sucked big…" Unfortunately before Gabe had the opportunity to explain to Rich the actual size of the suckage, the bathroom door exploded open catching the entire right side of Gabe's face and part of his shoulder. He fell to his knees, both hands simultaneously shooting up to cover where the door had creased his head.

"What the hell dude?" Rich stood in shock for a moment with his arms out like he was expecting a hug.

The heavyset Latino man wearing the black leather vest side-stepped the two and smirked as he passed. His knee brushed against Gabe's shoulder making shoot a hand out to the opposite wall to steady himself, "Do you *not* see me here bleeding? An apology would be cool."

As he passed, Rich got a much better look at their hallway companion and his bravado deflated. He was short and thick, but not fat. Rich could see the top of his head as he got closer. He could also see that the man was packed with muscle. He kind of reminded him of a mule. An old, mean tough mule. A mule who had no problem wearing a leather vest with no shirt on underneath. The vest identified him as the VP of the Desert Devils Motorcycle Club. His name was stitched on a patch on the front.

"*Miggie*". Rich startled himself and flinched at the sound of his own voice. He didn't mean to say it out loud. At the sound of his name Miguel snapped his eyes up to meet the skinny white-boy's. Rich froze. Miguel leaned in and got uncomfortably close. So close the smell of his sharply spiced cologne and hair oil made Rich's eyes water a bit. Three agonizing seconds passed, then the corner of Miguel's mouth twitched up in a smirk and he shot a short, condescending laugh out of his nose.

Gabe started to gather himself and Miguel simply turned and walked out into the bar.

"What…The… Hell?" Gabe mumbled through his hand.

Rich put an arm under his friend's elbow and helped him to his feet, "Let's go champ. I think you really got him."

"Shut up."

"No really, I really think he'll think twice before coming down this hallway again." Gabe could hear the smile in Rich's voice.

"Dude seriously… Shut Up," Gabe moaned.

"Okay fine, last one…" Rich pleaded. Gabe sighed, turned around and looked at Rich with his one open eye and waited for the closer, "I mean that vicious head-butt to the door would have struck fear into anyone. I know I was terrified. He's probably warning his," he made quote fingers in the air, "*Boys* right now."

"I hate you. Feel better?" Gabe asked.

Rich's smile widened, "Yes. Yes I do."

"Good. Glad I could brighten your day. Can we go look at my face now please?" The two made their way into the bathroom. The smell of stale urine and mold were almost overwhelming.

Gabe examined his tender face in the cracked mirror. "I am going to have a black eye."

"You did make-out with the edge of a door. What'd you expect?" Came Rich's voice from the stall. He flushed, came out and nudged Gabe over so he could wash his hands.

"Have I told you that I hate you today?"

Rich flicked the water from his fingers and ran his hands through his hair, "Yup."

Ω

"Where is our waitress?" Brian asked as he obnoxiously

scanned the bar. "It's been like twenty minutes since she took our order. How hard is it to make a hamburger?"

"Well she's not actually making it. You know that right?" Conner offered back.

"Well yah, but… shut up. You know what I mean." His eyes widened with recognition when he caught her over by the kitchen window. "Excuse me! DOR-IS! Can you please check on my order?"

Doris was a tall woman. She had long, thin black hair that continually fell out of the clip she tried to keep it up with. It was sort of an initiation when enjoying a meal at The Rusty Spoke to have the unpleasant experience of flossing a strand of Doris's locks out of your mouth from between your teeth.

It had been eight hours since Doris started her shift. She was pulling a double and she was nursing one hell of a hangover. She was going to be damned if some snot-nosed, rude, lily white yuppie punk was going to talk down to her today.

"You'll get it when you get it! I've got two hands!" She barked back before sticking her head in the kitchen window to talk to the line cook; presumably to tell him to add an extra helping of mucus to order number fourteen's burger. At least that's what was going through Conner's mind as he watched her.

He slapped Brian in the back of the head, "Seriously? Look around you moron. We don't quite fit in around here and I'd like to leave in one piece."

"I'm not being rude, I would just like my food at some point today," he said as he rubbed the spot where Conner had high-fived his skull. Steven laughed and flicked an ice cube from his water across the table into Brian's lap.

"Where are those two idiots? I want to get back on the road." Conner asked he looked toward the bathrooms.

"I don't know about them, but holy crap… look at the dude by the door," Steven said as he subtlety pointed with a finger held up by his cheek.

The other two turned around on their stools. Miguel had

joined a group by the side door next to the opposite bar.

"You mean the guy in the vest?" Brian asked.

"Yeah, in *just* the vest," Steven answered with raised eyebrows.

Ω

Miguel leaned against the bar and rubbed at the thick scar that ran from his left ear along his jaw to his chin; a memento he carried from a disagreement his club had with the Ender 31's. A year ago the other local bike club thought that he and five of his brothers should spend some time in the hospital for riding down a street in their territory. Miguel and his boys thought differently, so they hashed it out. A tire iron ended Miguel's voice in the dispute and he ate through a tube for two months.

At the moment, he was recanting his story of busting some goofy white-boy in the face with the bathroom door to one of his lieutenants. They must have been a long way from home. The other kid got brave for about two seconds before he realized where he was. He shut up real quick.

It was at that moment that he looked up and across the bar and saw the rest of those Casper-looking fools pointing and staring right at him. This just wouldn't do. Not in his bar.

Ω

Hand in the cookie jar. Deer in the headlights. Whatever analogy you wanted to use, that's what they were. To everyone's horror just as they all settled their judging gazes on the large man in the black vest, he snapped his eyes up and gave them all reason to find something else very interesting and very immediate to do.

Brian and Steven both found something intriguing on the floor and studied it with laser focus. Conner was suddenly struck with a powerful yawn that contorted his entire body like a yoga instructor to the point where he was facing the opposite direction on the stool.

"Well... he didn't look too friendly," Steven said, still looking at his shoe.

"Friendly, angry, homicidal... whatever. Same difference," Brian replied.

Conner looked at the two, "Yeah, so we should probably be moving along then. Where are those two idiots?"

Brian looked up, "Speak of the devil."

Gabe and Rich came walking out of the hallway behind them at a pretty good pace. Gabe had a wad of wet paper towels slapped over his right eye.

Conner turned to look at them, "What happened to winky over here?"

Rich turned to Gabe, "Shall I, or do you want to?"

"Go ahead," Gabe sighed.

"So... toughness over here decides he's had enough of doors and he..."

"Shut-up!" Gabe said cutting him off. "We were walking down the hall and some idiot throws the door open and destroys my face. Its killing me." He lowered the paper towels revealing an already black-and-blue halo around his eye.

"I think it's an improvement." Steven offered.

"It actually makes you less horrible to look at," Brian added.

Gabe grabbed an ice cube out of Steven's water, wrapped it in his paper towel and plopped it back on his eye, "I hate all of you."

Rich sat down on an empty stool, "But seriously, the guy was straight out of a low budget biker movie. Leather vest... no shirt. Who does that?"

Conner spoke without moving his lips all the while flicking his eyes over Rich's shoulder, 'That guy? That terrifying man over by the other bar?"

Rich spun to see, "Yeah! That guy right there."

Conner nudged him with his knee, "Don't stare! We gotta go."

Gabe dropped his makeshift eye-patch and blinked hard, "Oh yeah, that's him. Guy was unreal. Just a total meathead A-hole."

Conner firmly cupped Rich's arm, "Don't start anything. In case you haven't noticed we're a little outnumbered."

"The guy hit me in the face!" Gabe said as he threw down the wad of wet paper.

Steven tapped the table, "Hey guys?"

Conner then kicked his diplomacy up a notch and grabbed a fist-full of Rich's shirt, "Listen, don't be an idiot. Now's not the time."

"You didn't see what happened. It was unreal," he said as he twisted and broke free of the grip.

"Look at my face!" Gabe added with a finger slowly circling his swelling eye."

Steven slapped the table with two open palms like a toddler throwing a dinner-time tantrum, "Guys! Hey look at me!"

Conner, Gabe and Brian all snapped their attention back at Steven's request, "What?"

"We should really leave… now," Steven said as he motioned with his nose behind them.

"Oh my God we're in an episode of Son's of Anarchy," Everyone turned around at the sound of Rich's voice.

The group by the opposite bar had all stood and were headed over toward where the small group of five were sitting.

Ω

"Dude… seriously?" Conner looked over at Gabe, "What did you do?"

"Nothing. I've been right here with you, you ass." He replied.

The five friends slowly inched their way to the opposite side of the table and formed a small semi-circle. Brian looked longingly to his left and saw the door. Oh how he wished he could just be outside; away from all of this, away from the nightmare that was slowly approaching them.

To their right the neon *"Pisser"* sign flashed it's pale red message of relief over the dark hallway and somewhere behind them Doris was at the kitchen window picking up an order of Garlic fries and a cheeseburger (no onion) for a rude little punk on table fourteen.

The bar itself was about forty feet long. It ran the entire length of the building along the opposite wall from where the five were now huddled. Behind them was the kitchen where Doris had just departed from with a full tray of food on her shoulder, and a small dance floor that had been laminated into a back corner.

Beer logos, posters of bikini clad women, old bull skulls and a few biker insignias adorned the walls and ceiling immediately surrounding the drinking counter, giving it a rough rustic feel.

Brian found himself studying the décor of the establishment rather than focusing on the impending doom that had now crossed over half the distance to reach them. His brain was trying to trick him into believing that this was a movie, he was an actor, they were on a set and soon… very soon a director would yell *"Cut"* and tell everyone what a great job he did and how appreciative he was to work with such a group of professionals.

He took a deep breath and blinked hard, *"Come on,"* he told himself, *"Kids from suburbia only go into scary biker bars and get into Donny-brook fist-fights with leather clad motorcycle clubs in the movies."* Only this wasn't a movie, and the man with the scar on his chin was looking right at him.

Ω

Carl was a tall slender man. He had midnight black hair that fell to his shoulders which made his already slender face look absolutely gaunt. His right arm was completely sleeved in an eclectic array of inked artwork ranging from bare-breasted women, to tribal art, to what looked like a list of names with red lines cut through the middle of them. His left arm carried a quarter-inch thick scar that ran from his elbow to a nub of flesh that once anchored a ring-finger.

He grabbed the lapels of his denim vest and straightened it on his shoulders with a quick tug. The picture of a large bloodied fist with *"Southender 31"* embroidered around the knuckles centered itself in the middle of his back.

He watched the group of nine rise from the bar and slowly make their way over where the nervous group of white boys stood shoulder to shoulder facing them.

"It's about to pop off," he said to the two men standing behind him. The three had quietly slipped in a side door.

"Tell them all we're gonna do this here and now." He said as he motioned with an errant hand to the parking lot. The two men nodded and headed outside and returned a moment later with five new companions.

The eight watched the nine fan out around the table where the skittish white-boys were standing. They heard the first heated exchange between the two groups.

Carl looked over at a short tank-of-a-man, "You best earn your patch today Micky."

Micky grimaced and rolled his neck cracking a chorus line of bones. It sounded like popcorn cooking. He rubbed his shaved head like one would rub the exposed gut of a statue of Buddha for good luck and flicked open a serrated blade.

"It's on," he said through clenched teeth and they headed into the bar.

Ω

Gabe nervously eyed his friends then decided to take on the role of group mouthpiece, "Hey fellahs. Sooo… what's up?"

Miguel stood silent for a moment, "Where you from?"

Conner elbowed Gabe in the ribs making him wince then directed his attention to the group of nine, "We're just on our way to Vegas. Just stopped to get something to eat."

"For some out-of–towners you sure walk around here like you own the place." Miguel said as he rubbed his hands together and cracked his thick knuckles.

Conner put up his hands like he was trying to stop traffic, "Look we're sorry if you think we were acting disrespectful, we just…" his mouth clapped shut when Rich threw down his wad of wet paper towels. The flat moist thump it made when it hit the table drew everyone's attention for a second. "Look at my face! Seriously dude? My eye is jacked! How about a simple apology?"

Miguel slowly let his gaze fall on each of the five, "Here's what you're gonna get. An old-school beat down. Who the hell do you think you are coming into *my* bar and talking like you should be doing anything other than looking at the floor and saying yes sir?"

Steven counted nine men surrounding them in a semi-circle. He slowly began to inch backward. He wanted to be able to clearly see all nine men at once in his field of vision. Miguel continued his anger filled diatribe as Steven almost imperceptibly slid toward the back wall.

He didn't notice the edge of the table at first when it gently touched his thigh. The sound of the silverware scratching toward the edge reached his ears too late for him to do anything about it. It spun on its circle base like a drunkard about to cash it in for the night then toppled. The sharp crack of the Formica table-top hitting the ground was the starting pistol to the most horrible three minutes and seven seconds of Steven's twenty years, eleven months, three weeks and six days on Earth to date.

Ω

Doris jumped back at the sound of the crashing table

sending the contents of her tray skidding and splashing to the ground. As the four others turned around to see what had made the noise, Brian's hand hit the rim of one of the beer mugs sitting on the edge of the table next to them.

The man who happened to be standing to Miguel's left, stood, arms out, like the Karate Kid before a Crane-Kick examining his beer drenched lower half. He raised his head and balled his fists, "Mutha!"

Brian never saw the hit that sent him slamming face-first to the ground.

Ω

Bedlam ensued…

Ω

Brian had just craned his neck to see what the startling noise was when everything went a blistering white. He lay on the ground face-down, fighting for consciousness. He frantically blinked and tried to wipe away the blinding starbursts that were exploding behind his eyes like the Fourth-of-July finale.

Time froze and the four stood in shocked silence staring at their bleeding friend. The world rocketed back to pace when a hand grabbed the back of Rich's shirt and yanked him off of his feet like a limp marionette into the crowd. Three heads whipped around to see what Rich had screamed about in time to see a wall of bodies rushing them. The three tensed and began to battle for their lives.

Hands grabbed, and fists connected to elbows rained down like hail. Gabe fell to a knee and a steady stream of snot fired out of his nostrils like cake frosting when the knee crashed into his ribs. Robby, one of Miguel's lieutenants grabbed the stupid white boy by his hair and drew his knee back again, loading it like a spring. Gabe grabbed the hands woven into his hair tensed for the rib cracking blow.

Robby was thinking about how good it was going to feel when he broke this kid in two when he looked off to his right like he heard something intriguing off in the distance. Gabe pulled off one of his hands and looked up at his attacker. Panicked surprise flashed across his face. He drew in a long ragged breath and when he exhaled, thick foam the color of Doris's crimson lipstick came laboring out.

Bone scraped as Micky pulled the four-inch blade he was holding in his left hand out of Robby's back, just below the shoulder blade. He was earning his stripes today.

Robby fell forward and let go of the side of Gabe's head. Gabe now on all fours took no time to question why the large man who had told him that he was going to kill him was now lying on the ground exhaling Cool-Aid. He was focused on Rich. His friend was curled into the fetal position trying to protect his face and vital organs from two pairs of motorcycle boots. He made a beeline for him.

Ω

Carl saw the hit that sent the blonde white-boy to the ground, and by the time two of Miguel's boys grabbed the taller one and pulled him off his feet to the ground near the bathroom hallway they were within feet. They never saw them coming.

Ω

The eight attacked the nine who were attacking the five. Curses, bellows of pain and anger and the flat snaps of fists hitting flesh filled the already smoke filled room. Chairs broke, tables toppled, glass shattered and on the ground backlit by the dull flash of the neon "*Pisser*" sign, Rich opened his eyes just long enough to see Gabe half stumbling, half galloping on his hands and knees like a horse rounding the final curve at

Churchill Downs toward him.

He squeezed his eyes shut in preparation for the next kick to his already broken ribs when... it never came.

Ω

Gabe never bragged about his football career. He had no reason to. He played his Freshman year of high school. He was actually more, just on the team, than a player. He spent most of his time cheering on his teammates from the sidelines or from the bench where he would help fill up the water bottles for his exhausted friends.

He had a feeling that if his coach could have seen the hit he laid on the two men trying to stomp a hole through the middle of Rich's chest, he may have seen a little playing time. With a lowered shoulder and balled fists Gabe slammed into the two men from the side, folding them both in half at the waist like lawn chairs.

They fell into the hallway in a heap of leather and chains. The sound two skulls make when they crack together is very similar to what you get when one hits a coconut with an aluminum baseball bat. They didn't move again.

"Get up, get up, get up!" Gabe stammered as he pulled Rich's arm up and around his neck and shoulders to help him to his feet.

Rich winced as Gabe stood. "Ahh easy man! I think something's broken."

Gabe surveyed the mob looking for a familiar face. He saw Steven over by the bar where he was fighting to get someone to let go of his shirt.

Ω

Rich screamed something Conner couldn't quite understand. When he whipped his head around to see why his friend was practicing a new frantic language he was greeted with a wall of men in black leather vests rushing him. He caught the first one to make their way around the table by the Adam's-apple and the hair, and twisted his body to the left, sending the man head-first into a support beam that was several feet away.

There was no thought involved, just instinctual reaction. Hands, fists, place-settings, chairs; Conner wind-milled as he backpedaled. He wasn't sure, but later on when he really thought about it, he may have stabbed someone in the back with a fork. It was all a blur.

A commotion behind the wall of attackers seemed to take some of the attention of Miguel's Band of Merry Derelicts away and that was fine with Conner. He saw Brian laying on the floor in a little pocket of open space trying to crawl out of the way. It was all so surreal. There was no way this was actually happening. A broken bottle top sliced into his knee as he knelt down and put a hand on Brian's back.

Ω

The sounds were crisp. The tinkling of broken glass raining onto concrete floors. The symphony of four dozen voices adding their own individual snippet of flavor to the chaos stew. The soft thump of a fist driving into a stomach was matched by the flat slap of knuckles meeting an expectant cheek.

Conner saw stars as he drew back after breaking someone's nose with his forehead. He was a hurricane of limbs, chairs, bottles; basically anything that was within reach.

The battle had drawn in almost everybody in the bar. The three construction workers who had stopped for a drink after work, the two friends who were sitting at table eighteen who never did get their plate of nachos; most everyone had been bumped, spilled on, cursed at, knocked over or randomly hit and were now retaliating in kind. Conner was swimming in bodies, fighting against the tide. Steven quietly shook on the floor, his back against the foot rail at the base of the bar.

Ω

Gabe and Rich both snapped their eyes to the left when they heard Conner scream Steven's name. They watched him pass through a hole in the crowd heading toward the bar.

"What the hell dude?" Rich asked in disbelief. "What the hell is happening?"

Gabe un-slung Rich's arm from around his neck like a scarf and set his elbow gently down on a nearby table top.

"I gotta go get them," he said slowly shaking his head.

"How?" Rich asked.

Gabe's demeanor shifted into assault mode as the decision solidified in his brain. "Go find Brian and get the car. I'm gonna go get Conner and Stevie."

Rich winced as he took a breath, "You sure?"

Gabe shot a finger into his friend's face making his eyes cross, "Just be outside and ready to burn." He turned and headed toward the main bar. He could hear Conner screaming.

Ω

"Stevie! Stevie! Oh thank God dude. You okay?" Relief washed over Gabe's face as he dropped down and knelt next to where Steven was slouched under the bar. He had regained some semblance of coherency and was at least conscious which was a step in the right direction.

He stared blankly at Gabe for a moment before reaching up and softly patting his cheek. His hand fell back into his lap like a wet noodle, and Steven studied it with a curious gaze as if he couldn't quite figure out what he was supposed to do with it.

"This isn't good," Gabe muttered to himself. Steven was in no shape to do much of anything on his own. "Okay bud, sack-o-potatoes time." Gabe reached down and grabbed one of Steven's arms by the wrist. With a quick squat and a shoulder shrug he had his friend across his back in a fireman's carry, and he made his way towards the door.

It was a long twenty feet and it was far from smooth sailing. Gabe ate a hard shot to his kidney from some faceless coward behind him. He dropped to a knee, but turned it into a power-lunge and kept moving.

Brian met him at the doorway and grabbed Steven and they both limped toward the running car. Gabe turned back around to start the second phase of his rescue mission when Conner came sliding out of the crowd towards him on his back. He kicked at the two men who followed and were trying to get hold of him.

A hand made a solid grip on Conner's ankle and pulled him back. The second man stepped forward and raised his leg getting ready to stomp out this lunatic who had ripped off most of his right ear, when the fat end of a pool-cue shattered across the bridge of his nose. Gabe felt the impact in his shoulder, that was defiantly a home run.

The man stumbled back into his friend as he sputtered out thick globs of dark red blood and garbled curses. Gabe let what was left of the cue in his hand fall to the ground, and he reached down and grabbed Conner by the back of the shirt and pulled him out of the bar.

The back door was open and waiting. Gabe fell in backwards and pulled his bleeding broken friend on top of him. The door slammed, tires spun and the wounded five took off into the warm hazy afternoon just as a few dazed patrons began to stagger out of the bar.

Ω

Rich cracked the windows and a sweet smelling desert breeze filled the car. Conner brushed some of Steven's hair out of his face with the palm of his hand. It was covered in blood.

"What the hell just happened?" Brian blankly asked the

car.

"I don't know dude," Rich choked on the end of his sentence as a coughing fit made him wince.

The blood on Conner's shirt had turned a deep brown, and had dried to a crispy crust that flaked off like dandruff when he moved. He gingerly peeled the sticky garment away from his chest and looked down the stretched neck hole. What he saw made his stomach turn and the world tiled on it's axis for a moment.

Starting at the bottom of his collar bone, it looked like someone had taken a fillet knife and opened up a valley of flesh that ran to just above his nipple. He could see the fatty tissue flowering out from just below his skin and some dark purple muscle beneath that. Blood seeped out in waves every time he moved.

A flood of nausea and light-headedness slammed into his core and he had to swallow hard and take in a slow, deep, determined breath to not vomit, and then pass out on top of his little brother, who was laying in his lap. A thick line of spittle hung out of Conner's mouth like a nylon rope as he stared at the back of the driver's seat.

"Uhh, Con? You alright man? How's your chest?" Gabe gently put a hand on Conner's shoulder. It was like he was afraid he would break if he touched him too hard.

Conner shook his head and squeezed his eyes shut, "Yah, I'm fine. I just don't feel very good."

Brian stopped rubbing the back of his head and turned around in the passenger seat. "You don't look very good."

Conner flicked his eyes up and looked at Brian from beneath his brows, "Thanks."

"No, seriously. That cut on your chest is bad and Steven isn't saying much. Look at the back of his head man."

Conner ran his finger-tips along the back of his little brother's head. A weak, surprised gasp escaped him when they found the soft tennis ball sized lump that had taken up residence behind his left ear. Steven stirred when Conner pressed a bit on the lump to see how bad it was and his eyes fluttered open.

"Water," Everyone fell silent, "I want some water."

"Okay buddy," Conner said. He looked up and angrily snapped his fingers at Brian, "Water! Find some!"

A frantic exploration erupted and of every inch of floor, seat, and cushion were scoured before Gabe yelled and held up a warm half-drunk bottle like it was an idol to be worshipped by some jungle tribe in the Amazon. Conner reached over and snatched it out of Gabe's hand. Blood began to pour from the portal into his sternum but he was too worried about Steven to notice.

"Hey turn your head buddy. Take a drink, " Conner tilted the bottle and poured a small stream into Steven's mouth. He coughed and most of the water poured into Conner's lap.

"Con?" Steven reached up and found Conner's face. "I don't feel good. My head hurts." With that he closed his eyes and a tremor racked his entire body like he'd grabbed a live wire.

"I know buddy," Conner fought back a lung crushing wave of panic that was rolling in like high-tide in from the outskirts of his mind. "Brian get on your cell and find us a damn hospital."

Ω

"Jeremy stop doing that. It's the last time I'm going to ask you." Gabby reached over and clamped a firm hand over her son's left leg to stop him from kicking the table in front of them. He had been doing it since they'd arrived, and he seemed to be getting a good deal of enjoyment from it. From the looks on the faces of their other unfortunate temporary roommates, he was the only one.

The man sitting to their left, who had sliced off most of his index finger with an infomercial Ginsu knife, kept shifting his sullen eyes from mother to child and back again. In fact, everyone in the waiting room had locked an icy, irritated gaze on the cause of the incessant knocking.

Gabby could feel them all trying to bore quarter sized holes into her skull with their eyes. It was quite uncomfortable. She wasn't a bad mother. She was just exhausted. She was up at three-thirty, out the door by four, to work a double, bagging at the Wal-Mart.

She pulled back into her driveway at seven in the evening to meet her husband and do the switch as he left for his night shift. That's when he informed her that Jeremy thought he had developed two of Superman's most popular abilities. Invulnerability and the power of flight. He tested both from the roof of the garage and was now holding his broken arm against his chest in a make-shift sling, while he tried to wiggle out of his mother's grasp to kick the edge of the table again.

Gabby was about to hurl another empty threat at her son when the automatic doors to the Emergency Room "*hissed*" open. Her gasp was intriguing enough to warrant a courtesy glance from the others currently gearing up to listen to the third act of "Stomp: Emergency Room Edition".

The five men who shuffled through the entrance belonged in the final scene of a World War Two drama, where the wounded hero and his brothers-in-arms would limp into frame and survey the eerily still battlefield after a hard fought and valiant victory over the Nazis'. The camera would pan their weathered, blood-caked faces as they drank in the carnage of some nameless devastated farmland in Southern France. The protagonist would say something both profound and quirky, and then the camera focus would soften and pan away to the setting sun leaving their fate to the imagination.

Yes, they belonged in a wartime drama, but this was an Emergency Room in the High Desert off Interstate Fifteen, and Jeremy didn't need revisit this tonight in some grotesque nightmare. Gabby reached over and cupped her hand over her son's eyes.

Shock and tension grew in the room in equal amounts as the five men made their way to the main nurse station. They limped, coughed, cursed and one carried another in his arms like a groom holds his bride crossing the threshold for the first time. When the charge nurse looked up from her computer screen the cat leapt out of the proverbial bag. She jumped to her feet and started barking orders into a microphone and pointing to nearby staff delegating assignments.

$$\Omega$$

"Please, please, please God, please," Conner rocked back and forth in the blue plastic chair he had taken from the hallway, "Please let him be alright."

Steven had been unconscious for the past nine hours. The doctor had told him that preliminary tests had confirmed a moderate amount of swelling on his brain from the blunt force trauma he had suffered behind his ear.

Conner had spent a few hours getting the valley of flesh someone had carved into his chest closed. Thirty stitches later he found his way back to his baby brother's room. Brian, Rich and Gabe had been X-Rayed, stitched and interviewed by the police. Earlier that evening they all said their goodbyes, gave their well-wishes and left for home.

He was alone. He sat and stared at Steven's chest as it rose and fell. He found himself counting his breaths. Questions began to swirl themselves into his mind. They were questions he had tried so hard to block out. Unfortunately he could only hold that door closed for so long, and those questions finally kicked the frame away from the hinges and came smashing through his soul. They kept coming, and coming, and coming until he felt as if he were drowning. It was hard to breathe.

"What if my baby brother dies? Was it my fault? Could I have stopped it?" Then the tone of his internal dialogue changed. It grew dark like the sky when the sun is swallowed by a cloud bank.

"Of course it was my fault. He's my baby brother, it was my job to protect him. I failed him. I failed! I should have been able to get to him sooner! I shouldn't have let him get hurt in the first place!" Conner felt a twinge of the blind rage that had taken control of him earlier and his chest tightened. He balled his fists and doubled over in the chair.

"You failed! Your little brother is going to die and it's all your fault! You were weak and selfish and slow! You never really loved him much!" Conner grabbed two fistfuls of hair on either side of his head and reared back in agony, almost folding the plastic back of the chair in half.

He was going to pass out. Spots danced and chased each other in a schizophrenic game of tag in front of his eyes. A high pitched wailing sound began to build in his ears and quickly reached a screaming crescendo. He'd had anxiety attacks before, but this was different. This was world ending. It felt like the apocalypse of his soul… like he was dying. It was as if there were something actually trying to kill him.

His face throbbed as the blood hammered behind his ears. A bitter, metallic taste flooded his mouth and stung his throat. The barrage of evil, hateful thoughts quickened their pace and Conner felt himself going over the edge. Blame, regret, hate; he should just kill himself rather than live with the guilt of his brother dying. How would he explain it to his parents when they arrived? How? Just end it. Nothing will ever be the same! He could hear them… literally hear them.

Just as he was about to give up; poised to drop off into the abyss that had formed in his mind, a new thought squeaked through and found it's way into the mix. It was so quiet and small that Conner was lucky he didn't miss it. Something from a dream he had months ago, and had almost forgotten shone through the darkness.

At first, it was like a single candle set at the end of a very dark cave, barely visible, "*I will always be with you. Believe.*"

His fear fueled self destruction would have nothing to do with it. "Believe that you got your baby brother killed!" This time it was stronger, brighter; a spotlight in the darkness, "Believe that you did all you could. God is with you."

Conner slid his hands down his face and balled them into

his shirt and some of the gauze from his chest dressing. His gaze locked happenstance onto the railing of Steven's bed and focused on it with a fierce determination as he fought through each painful breath.

He wanted to rebut the new voice; tell it why he deserved every searing, horrible moment of this new agony. Before he could muster a counter-argument the voice came through with such power and volume that it simply reached critical mass and went supernovae in his brain. It shone like a thousand suns through the blackness, illuminating every hidden corner of doubt and evil in his mind. It turned the night of his soul into blazing mid-day... blinding, "Believe In Me And I Will Never Leave You!"

Ω

Conner leaned back and threw out his chest as he took a deep releasing breath. It was as if the giant invisible fist that had been crushing his sternum had throw open it's hand. His father had been in Vietnam and had told him once that everyone temporarily converted to Christianity in the middle of a fire-fight. They were called foxhole Christians. Death and pain always seem to serve as great catalysts for religious epiphanies.

So far that had been the pattern of Conner's life. He would mosey along and do whatever came his way. Then tragedy would strike and lightening quick he was looking to the Heavens, asking God for a little assistance, wondering where He had been all this time. For the first time in his life this felt different. Conner felt a sense of peace wash over him like he were being lowered into a warm bath. This time it felt real. He felt compelled to pray; not out of fear and desperation, but out of love.

Rote prayers that he had learned in church as a child came stumbling out of his mouth at first. They were dry and mechanical. When he had exhausted the three he could remember he simply looked up at the ceiling and started to talk to God. There was no script. No rhyme or reason. There was just Conner's bare unashamed heart.

Genuine emotion materialized into tears that began to streak down his cheeks and drip off of the tip of his chin. Something felt wrong so he slid down to his knees. A small wince escaped his lips when he landed right where a bottle had cut him earlier. With hands clasped together in front of him, he began to let the Lord know how important it was that his little brother be alright.

"He's my baby brother. Just let it be me. Take me instead." Conner fought against the choking convulsions that threatened to rack his body but he was so tired. They came.

He put his face into the side of the bed by Steven's ribs and sobbed into the blanket. Every bit of emotion he hadn't been able to put into words came pouring out of him

Time passed; how long he had no idea. He may have fallen asleep for a little bit. It had been long enough to completely soak a head sized silhouette into the sheet, and seep a thin red line of now dried blood through the white shirt the nurse had given him.

He just looked around the room like he was seeing it for the first time. Absently studying it. With a quick shake of his head, Conner came back to himself and looked over at his brother. All of the horror and sorrow was gone. He wasn't sure if he was just exhausted, or maybe he'd had some deep spiritual revelation. He honestly had no idea. All Conner knew was that he could breathe, he didn't want to die, and looking at Steven didn't make him want to melt into a puddle of tears.

With a few awkward scoots, he worked himself back up into the chair and wiped his face with the bottom of his shirt. Months ago Conner had experienced something truly remarkable. He survived something when he rationally knew he shouldn't have. He'd had an incredibly moving dream that same night that shook him to his core. Made him question what he believed. But like with much in life, time heals all wounds and tends to make the old memory a tad bit fuzzy.

Conner wavered back and forth from a message from God to a crazy dream. From divine intervention to dumb, I just won the lottery luck. He wasn't sure if there was a God, or if there was, if He was listening right now but he figured there had to be something going on here, and it was worth a shot.

"Lord, if you are really there..." Conner smirked a little because he knew that what he was about to say had been said in a thousand corny movies, written in a thousand corny novels and forcefully said by a thousand corny flamboyant evangelists on cable television asking for his hard earned money; but he said it anyway.

He closed his eyes, "Lord, just give me a sign. Please... anything."

He opened one eye, then the other and peered around the room. Nothing. No peels of thunder or searing lightening ripped through the hallways. No unseen heavenly choir spontaneously erupted into a moving rendition of Glory, Glory Halleluiah, and no angel, with flaming sword in hand stood flexing majestic at the foot of Steven's bed. Nothing.

He leaned forward and rested his forearms next to Steven's leg. He would just wait for his parents to get there and talk to the doctors later. For now he would just have to... his heart jumped. Conner held his breath, and with wide disbelieving eyes he tried to process. Steven had reached over and lightly grabbed his wrist.

"Stevie? Can you hear me buddy?" Conner put his hand over his brother's and shook it. "Stevie! Look at me man! Look at me!" He didn't respond. He just kept on doing nothing, but it was enough for Conner.

"I don't know if that was you God, but if it was... it'll do. Thank you."

Ω

The swelling on Steven's brain stayed relatively constant over the next couple of days, but on Sunday August 24th three days after his twenty-first birthday, Steven woke up.

Conner and his family had rented a hotel room and stayed in the high desert. The doctors were against moving him in his unstable condition. Over those few days Conner and his parents spent as much time as they could by Steven's side; most of the time they were there as a unit. There were times when they would stay in shifts. It was on one of these occasions when Conner was alone with Steven, that another one of the veiled miracles which seemed to quietly slip into Conner's life like a crocodile slides unnoticed into a river crossing full of wildebeests, occurred.

It was early and the high desert skyline had gone from the deep black of night, to gray, to a soft blue and was currently beginning to show a light yellow tint as the sun rose in the East. Conner was in his sentry chair next to Steven's bed. He was reading and had been for the past three days. He turned the page and saw it was the last page of the book. The book of Psalms.

After his experience three days prior, when The Lord seemingly answered a small desperate prayer, Conner felt compelled to fulfill a promise he made to himself months earlier to actually read the Bible instead of using it as a drink coaster.

He had searched the room and the area around Steven's bed but he couldn't find a Bible.

He turned to Steven, "Isn't it a law or something that hospitals have to keep Bibles in every room? Or is that hotels?" He looked over at Steven and waited for an answer. He shrugged, "That's what I thought."

Frustrated, he blew a gust a air from his lower lip to move a bit of hair from his forehead.

"This sucks. What's a guy gotta do to..." before he could finish his thought the portly on-call nurse who had been assigned to Steven's room came popping through the door. She was a little ball-of-a-woman, with short stocky arms and legs like tree stumps. Her skin was the color of midnight and she kept her curly hair in a tight bun on the crown of her head that she constantly patted to make sure it was behaving.

"Hi there sweetie," she said with her deep southern accent and toothy smile stretching her kind face. She made Conner happy. That was the only way he could describe it. He was never much into the whole ethereal energy, chakra, mood crystal thing, but when Joanne came into the room he simply felt good.

"Hi Joanne. How're you?" Conner said with a small wave.

"Just fine honey. How's our little man?" She said absently looking at one of his monitors.

"The same I guess. He moved a little bit earlier."

"That's our little man isn't it now? Little fighter." She reassuringly rubbed Conner's arm as she passed.

"Hey Joanne… would you happen to know where I could find a Bible?" Conner sheepishly asked.

She spun to face Conner so quickly he was afraid she may fall over. She clapped her hands together in front of her mouth, "Well praise Jesus of course I do! I always have one with me in my bag. I'll go right quick and get it for you." She put her hands in the air and shook them like she were trying to flick water off of them, "It does my heart good to see a young man such as yourself interested in learning about our Lord and Savior Jesus Christ!"

She turned to leave and opened the door before hopping back, "I'll be right back quicker than grease skipping off a hot skillet." With that she disappeared into the hall. Conner could hear her happily humming to herself as she walked away.

He sat with his mouth half open, feeling like someone had just blown an air-horn in his ear, and then dunked him underwater. He was shocked. That was much more of a response than he had expected. A simple "*Sure*" would've suited him just fine. A few minutes passed and Conner heard the staccato *Pock* of Joanne's heels on the tiled hallway floor. She threw open the door and held the book over her head in reverence.

"I got it for you sugar." She cheered.

"Thanks Joanne, I really appreciate it," he replied.

"Not a word honey. I was happy to get it for you and you keep it as long as you need. Now you just spend time in the word and with our little man here. You know he can hear you? Maybe you read some to him too?" She said with a finger pointed at Steven.

Conner nodded and smiled.

Joanne absently reached up and gave her bun a good pat, "Okay then. God bless you." With that, she winked and was gone. Conner waited until he could no longer hear her heels echoing down the hallway before opening the book.

Ω

From that point on, over the next three days he read voraciously. He didn't know if it was the current trauma, or fear, or some genuine spiritual God-inspired motivation but he devoured chapter and verse. He came to the last Psalm, Psalm One-Fifty. It read:

"Praise the Lord God in his sanctuary; praise Him in His mighty heavens. Praise Him for His acts of power; praise Him for His surpassing greatness. Praise Him with the sounding of the trumpet; praise Him with the harp and the lyre; praise Him with the tambourine and dancing; praise Him with the strings and flute; praise Him with the clash of cymbals; praise Him resounding cymbals.

Let everything that has breath praise The Lord. Praise The Lord."

Conner sat back into the chair and stretched his neck. He rocked forward and let the book fall into his lap. His eyes burned and he was exhausted. He rubbed them with his palms like a child who needed a nap.

"Well… I guess I'll praise The Lord then," he said with a hint of tired sarcasm. The digital clock on the wall said it was six-fifteen in the morning. The sun had just broken the horizon and was spilling around the edges of the window shade. He needed to stretch and his knees popped as he stood.

The stale fluorescents had slowly been sucking the life out him and he felt like recharging in the sun. He slowly shuffled over to the window and grabbed hold of the cord.

"Rise and shine Stevie," he said half as a joke, half as a hidden prayer. With a quick pull of the string, the pure morning light of Sunday the twenty-fourth of August flooded the room.

It was bright. Much brighter than it should've been. Conner thought it was just because he had been in a dim hospital room for so long and his eyes hadn't adjusted yet, but he couldn't keep them open for more than a second at a time. He may have been evolving into a new mole-man species of hominid.

A few moments passed and the clock ran out on the normal amount of time it would take even a Cole-Miner's eyes to adjust to the sun after a double shift a mile deep, and panic set in. He held a hand to his face to try and shield it from the light but it didn't do any good. It was as if the light were coming from everywhere. He groped a blind hand over toward the window and found the cord and gave it solid tug. It was stuck.

During his struggle with the shades, he felt the air move around him like it does when someone rushes past you in close proximity. To be more accurate, it felt like a rhinoceros was doing wind sprints next to Steven's bed. He froze. Blind and confused, Conner's mind tried to find a rational explanation.

"Joanne? Joanne is that you? I can't see. I think something might be wrong my eyes."

There was no answer but Conner could definitely feel a presence in the room. It was heavy. That was the only way he could describe it.

"Joanne please..." He let go of the cord and took a timid step toward Steven's bed. All of the hair stood up on the back of his neck; the air was almost humming. He froze. Fear gripped his chest. He swore he heard a breath. A deep heavy breath.

"Steven? Buddy are you there?" He asked as he took another step. His thigh touched the edge of the bed. With a great deal of will and force he commanded his eyelids to open.

For a split second he saw a silhouette on the other side the bed opposite him. A massive silhouette.

Nothing made sense. Adrenaline exploded into his veins and he readied himself to leap blindly over the bed to try to protect his brother from whoever or whatever this was. He loaded, and took a last lung filling breath to ready himself, when the figure simply erupted with light. Conner recoiled in pain. He could see the white through his eyelids no matter how hard he squeezed.

"Let Everything That Has Breath Praise The Lord!" The voice boomed into existence from all sides and angles. Surround sound didn't begin to explain what he was experiencing. It felt like someone had put his head inside of a main-stage speaker at a Stone's concert and cranked the gain up to ten.

He flinched from the initial shock and fell back into the window. Conner was the light. It was beyond bright. It was beyond reason. It just was. He steadied himself on the wall with an outstretched hand and faced their visitor.

"What are you?" he asked.

"Believe." Came the reply.

Conner didn't know what else to do. The logical, rational side of his brain packed up shop and had gone home for the night. So he did the only thing he could think of. He stood with his arms out like he was waiting for a hug. He gave in.

"Con? Is that you?"

Conner's knees buckled at the sound of his brother's voice. When he hit the ground his eyes shot open. He could see. The light was gone and so was the visitor. His brother however was looking over the edge of the bed at him with a quizzical expression tacked on his face.

"Dude, are you alright?" Steven asked as he gingerly rubbed his head.

Conner shot to his feet and jumped on his brother like a spider monkey and hugged him.

"Con! Whoa! Take it easy dude. I'm sore" Steven winced as Conner pushed himself back to a seated position.

Once back, he grabbed either side of Steven's face and stared at him. "Oh my God. Oh my God. Oh my God, you're okay."

"Yah dude, I'm okay. How long was I asleep?" It sounded more like, "Howe ong washz I a sheep?" Because Conner had his face crushed between his hands but he got the gist.

Before Conner could tell him, Joanne burst through the door with a frantic look twisting her face, "What's happening babies? My little man's monitors went off the charts a second ago and…" She stopped mid-sentence when she saw Steven looking back at her from between Conner's hands.

"Heh-wowe…"

"Well hello my child." Joanne replied.

She looked from Conner to Steven and back again, "Well praise Jesus!" She erupted, "Our little man is awake!"

"You don't know the half of it Joanne," Conner said as he reached over behind Steven's back and hugged his brother.

Ω

Astonishing was the word the doctor used to describe Steven's instant recovery. The swelling had completely receded, the small skull fracture had healed; a CAT scan showed no precursors to scarring or permanent tissue damage to his brain.

"Steven is a very lucky young man." Dr. Lewis said as he set a metal clipboard down on the counter next to him.

The exam room they were in was a little cramped. It was cold and smelled of bitter antiseptic. Steven and Conner sat on the exam table while their parents took the chairs. Dr. Lewis reached down and grabbed the front of the stool he was on and scooted forward a bit.

"From what I can see," he looked at Steven, "You're going to be fine young man."

"I feel pretty good," Steven replied while he rubbed his head.

"Good. Good," Dr. Lewis picked up the clipboard and

flipped through a handful of pages. A perplexed look dropped down over his face like the curtain at a high school play.

Their father Mike took the bait, "Is there something else? You look concerned."

Dr. Lewis flipped a few more pages and dropped the clipboard in his lap. "Mr. and Mrs. Parker, I am a medical professional and I like to think that I am fairly well respected in my field. I can only comment on what I know, and what the results of the tests we've administered show me."

He opened his hands palms up in a questioning gesture, "This is my sixteenth year as an emergency medical resident and I have no explanation for your son's recovery. There is nothing in the books to explain how the swelling vanished overnight with no residual effects. The human body simply cannot reabsorb blood that quickly. And," he gestured with a flip of his hand to Steven to lean forward. Steven complied and Dr. Lewis ran a finger along a small bump behind his ear, "The Osteoblasts, the bone growing cells in the body should not have been able to heal this fracture so quickly."

He leaned back and rubbed his chin, "Steven shows what looks like over a years worth of bone growth on that crack in his skull."

Mike looked over at Sarah then at his children before standing up and extending his hand to Dr. Lewis, "Well I don't know how you did it Dr. but thank you."

Dr. Lewis stood and grasped Mike's hand, "On the record, I'm glad that I, along my hard working and dedicated staff here at St. Joseph's Memorial could provide you and your family with exemplary care and service." He then clasped his other hand over the top of their obligatory handshake and pulled himself into Mike's personal bubble.

He dropped his voice a few decibels and looked skittishly around the room for dramatic effect, "Off the record, I had nothing to do with your son's recovery and that's the truth. I simply made him comfortable. This is one for the books to be filed under I have no freaking idea but I'll take it." He shook his head and smirked, "I don't know if you're a religious man but you may have someone else to thank." With that he slowly raised his eyes upward. Mike slowly followed his gaze until they were both staring quizzically at the ceiling.

Ω

Conner sat in the car with his forehead against the window. It was cool against his skin and it felt good. With his little brother sitting next to him and his parents up front, it felt like they were on a family trip back when they were kids.

He liked that feeling. It let him escape from the reality of what had happened over the past couple of days. He thought about the hospital room a thousand times over. Every possible explanation; every angle; every last "*what if*" scenario had been proposed, analyzed and shot down.

He drew his head back and let it thump against the glass. The light. The voice. There was no way that could be it. No way. But there was no other rational, logical way to wrap his mind around what he experienced. It was like Sherlock Holmes said, "Once you eliminate the impossible, whatever remains, no matter how improbable, must be the truth." He closed the search browser on his iPhone. He knew there had to have been a quote about that out there somewhere.

Conner turned and looked at Steven. A small puddle of drool had collected on his right shoulder as he slept.

"I saw an angel?" he questioningly whispered at his brother. Then defiant disbelief welled up in his chest and he scoffed, "I saw… an an-gel." Then fear washed over his face, "I saw an angel?" He let that feeling hang over him for a moment until the realization set in.

He snapped his eyes up and locked them on Steven. He grabbed his brother's shoulder and shook him awake.

"Wha, whaderyoudoing?" Steven slurred still half asleep.

"I. Saw. An. Angel." Conner demanded.

Steven was quiet for a few moments as the shroud lifted from his mind. "Huh?"

"I saw an angel," he repeated with the same ferocity.

Steven sheepishly pointed out the window, "On the freeway?" He said through a yawn. "Did his car break down?"

Conner shook his head, "No, yesterday."

A slow methodic nod began to move Steven's head like he was keeping time to a song only he could hear, as he thoughtfully pouted his lower lip, "I see. Okay. An angel. Like a," he held out his arms and flapped his hands like little wings, "An Angel?"

"Yes."

He then joined his fingers and thumbs in a ring and held them above his head like a halo, "Like, an angel?"

Conner's voice dropped an octave, "Yes…"

A small smirk played at the corner of Steven's mouth. He did his best to mime a harp while doing a pretty decent Ray Charles impression, "An… Angel?"

Conner's fist fired out like a piston and connected with Steven's shoulder. They both recoiled in pain. Conner from the bruised knuckles he had on both hands, and Steven from the body bruise he was nursing.

"Dude! Seriously?"

"I'm sorry!" he said shaking his wrist. "If it makes you feel any better I think my knuckles are broken."

"Kind of. Dude just let me go back to sleep. We'll talk about your fairies, or goblins, or angels when we get home." With that Steven shut his eyes and let his head fall against the rest. Conner did the same.

He thought back to what Joanne had said after she bounded into the room and found Steven awake.

"The Lord Jesus is good indeed honey. Look at this, by His grace my little man is alright and his big brother is right there loving on him." She walked over and enveloped them both in a strong meaty embrace. She smelled like peppermint mouthwash and hand sanitizer. For some reason it was comforting. "The Lord must have something special planned for you two. My two little babies."

V. Nicholas Gerasimou

CHAPTER 4

THE FIVE TIME: BEHIND THE VEIL

V. Nicholas Gerasimou

THE FIVE TIME:
BEHIND THE VEIL

Fate and predestination, verses the happenstance theories of chance and dumb luck, are difficult topics for humans to wrap their finite minds around. For instance, if one chose to have a turkey sandwich for lunch on a given particular Wednesday afternoon at four thirty-six in the p.m., in a Subway Sandwich Shop; why did they pick turkey?

Did they choose it because the Lord had predetermined before time immemorial that on that day, at that exact time, in that exact restaurant, seated in that particular booth, wearing that exact shirt; that they would order, eat, and enjoy a turkey sandwich on rye with Swiss, mayo, lettuce, a dill pickle, salt, pepper and two strips of extra crispy bacon and a diet Coke or the world would stop spinning? Or, did they just not feel like the roast beef?

Being a messenger of light for The Lord God Almighty, Sariel had a bit more insight into the matter than his mortal charge did. That knowledge still did little to temper the fear and anger he simultaneously felt as he raised his sword to block a rage filled high-guard attack from above.

The two blades met with a shower of sparks. The sound of angelic steel, denting demonic metal, bit sharply through the air. Sariel spun low and simultaneously lunged forward ducking under his foe's recoiling blade. A clean powerful swipe rendered the demon in two at the waist.

He stood and surveyed the bar. The room was chaos. Demon's clung greedily to the backs of dozens of leather clad men as they slew each other. Man, angel, and demon were clashing in an epic battle which ironically only spanned the width of the small, insignificant bar they all found themselves in.

The five were fighting for their lives, and Sariel along with his trusted group of brothers were doing their best to keep them alive. Parrying, dodging, hacking, slashing; once again he found himself doing the very thing he believed The Lord had created him for. To protect those made in His image from the Evil One.

A cry of anger and sorrow ripped Sariel's attention toward the bar. Adriel, the one who had been charged with watching over and protecting Steven stood on the bar above where the young man had just fallen. He stood to his full height, head scraping the ceiling, and with a powerful flash flung his wings out to full extension. He was simultaneously majestic and terrifying. With a loud sorrow filled cry, he leapt into the swarm of black wraiths below him and carved out an area of open space around where Steven lay.

Sariel saw it all happen, and when Conner made his move to reach his baby brother he was already in the air. He landed straight in Conner's path, and like a lead blocker taking care of linebackers for the ball carrier, Sariel simply bowled over anyone, demon or not, in his way.

Conner knelt by Steven's side, blood pouring from his chest but alive. It was almost time to leave. He looked up and saw that Brian and Rich had made their way outside to get the car as they should have. He just had to protect them for two more minutes before they were all out of danger.

Conner surged into the crowd and Sariel followed like his shadow. As they left his side, Adriel dropped over Steven like a wet blanket. He looked up and saw Gabe making his way toward them. Good. Very good.

Ω

The car tires spun and crunched in the gravel, peppering the wood paneled facade of the bar as they made their escape. They were battered, bruised and bleeding… but alive. Sariel and the others kept pace around the sedan like a flying angelic police motorcade.

The lights were all green as they made their way towards the hospital.

Ω

Sariel had trouble understanding what The Lord had told him. He did not question it, and he would carry out his orders with glory and thanks, but the nature of the order confused him. He was to let the enemy have access to Conner. He was told to let one of the fallen directly speak to, and influence the boy in this time of sorrow and need.

Conner sat next to Steven's bed in a flimsy blue plastic chair and prayed. Sariel stood in the far corner of the room and watched like a stone sentry. Unmoving, his face was a picture of stern disapproval, and when he sensed them, hatred. They came like a cold wind, sneaking into the room through the cracks.

Three of them stood next to Steven's bed. Conner on one side, they on the other. The one closest to the head leaned over Steven's face and smiled a wide sick smile. He brought a twisted gray finger up and slowly ran it along Steven's forehead, like one does to test the cleanliness of a tabletop after it's been dusted. Instantly Ardiel appeared, sword in hand, eye's ablaze ready for battle.

Sariel quieted him with a stern look and an apologetic shake of his head. The demon left his finger on Steven's cheek and turned his head at an impossible angle so he could see the boy's guardian behind him. A shrill chatter-like laugh rattled out of his chest at the sight of the rage filled Angel. Adriel turned to his commander, and with pain in his eyes, begged.

"Please Sariel! Allow me to stop this perversion."

Sariel shut his eyes and dropped his head, "The Lord wills it brother. Have faith."

Adriel sheathed his sword and took a spot next to Sariel near the back wall.

The demon closest to the foot of the bed turned and faced them.

"Hello brothers. It has been too long."

Sariel flicked his eyes up and locked them on the empty black orbs looking back at him, "Do not call us that. You lost the right to call us brother long ago."

"Oh, so it's a right now is it?" He nudged the one standing next to him and made a sarcastic show of waving his arms like he were bowing to royalty, "A... privilege."

His demeanor instantly darkened like the sky before a hurricane, "You think you have any power over us? You think I answer to you!" He flipped back the wet leathery drape of his cloak and produced a crooked, rusty dagger.

Sariel's grip on the hilt of his sword tightened and he swallowed the impulse to explode across the room and send all three screaming into the abyss.

Instead Adriel stepped forward, "Beleth. Stop this." Desperation danced on the edge of every word.

"So you do remember me... brother? He asked with a smirk as he playfully waved the blade over Steven's motionless body.

"Of course we do," Sariel flatly answered. "We know each and every one of you as we once did in the Kingdom. But your betrayal has stripped you of the right to be called as one of us."

"Hmm... betrayal." The word dripped off of his gray leathery lips like hot wax. He turned to face the angels and squared himself. "Betrayal?" With a flick of his shoulders the meat like garment that was draped over his shoulders fell to the ground with a wet slap.

It was as if he'd been slouching, because as Beleth raised his head he simply expanded. Thick coils of dark muscle writhed beneath his scarred ash covered skin. He rose and the crown of his head met a light fixture above him making it flicker.

What stood before Sariel and Adriel was a monster in every sense of the word. The stuff of nightmares that haunted the dreams of mortals. Locks of dark twisted hair fell in ropes to Beleth's waist. He brushed them aside with a curled hand sporting talons each the size of a butcher's meat hook. Sinew, bone and muscle wove themselves into a massive schizophrenic tapestry of hate and rage.

"Betrayal!" Spittle flew from Beleth's mouth in a fine mist. His purple tongue raked across rows of razor-sharp sharks teeth. "You know nothing of betrayal! Shunned! Cast out into the darkness! To live here!" He turned and angrily flung an arm in Conner's direction, "With them!" The other two demons flinched back at their companion's fury. "For simply questioning the All Mighty… I was thrown away. Forever."

Sariel dropped his hands from his sword and stepped forward, "You know as well as I do you did more than question. You fought in the rebellion with Lucifer. Against me. Against Him."

Beleth stepped back and seemed to deflate. He nodded and stroked his head thoughtfully with a claw. "Him," he let the word hang in the air for a moment. "Him. Him. Him." He nodded, turned and walked around the foot of the bed, stopping above Conner's quivering shaking form. "Speaking of," he shot a talon upward, "Him. Speaking of Him, I happen to know that I've been granted access to this one." With that he turned to Conner and gently placed a hand on the nape of his neck. Instantly, Conner's breathing became labored and shallow.

On instinct, Sariel unsheathed his sword. The heat of holy fire burned in his eyes. "Not to harm!"

Beleth turned to his righteous brother and with a look

that a loving parent gives a small child when asked why Mr. Bubbles stopped swimming and has taken up an exciting new career as a buoy said, "Oh no dear brother. Of course not. Never harm. I am simply here to help. I want to help this young man get through his time of need and sorrow."

Adriel put and hand on Sariel's shoulder and drew him back. "Have faith brother. Have faith the Heavenly Father knows best."

He nodded and sheathed his sword. "His ways are perfect. He is always faithful." It was as if he were reassuring himself, and as he did a sense of calm washed over him. He retook his post at the back of the room standing guard. Waiting.

"Amen." They both said in unison.

Ω

Beleth leaned over Conner like a dark umbrella, "What if your baby brother dies? It would be all your fault."

Sariel continued a silent prayer to the Lord as he watched the demon pour lies into Conner's heart. The other two evil beings leaned over Steven's motionless body and yelled blasphemous threats into his sleeping mind. Adriel rolled his massive neck and looked away. It was all he could do to control himself.

"It was all your fault! You failed him! You failed yourself! You were weak and selfish and slow! You never really loved him!" Pleasure and satisfaction flashed in equal amounts across Beleth's face.

Conner reared back in his chair almost folding the back in half. Agony filled his eyes and escaped his lips in labored sounds as he fought for breath. Sariel shut his eyes and lowered his head.

Beleth placed a scaled hand in the middle of Conner's chest, "You will never be able to live with yourself when he dies. How will you tell your parents? They will blame you, you know that. Nothing will ever be the same. Ever."

Conner's face had gone from a candy-apple red to a pallid off white. The sorrow was contorting his body into unnatural positions. Sariel looked skyward and obediently waited for his prayer to be answered, Adriel did the same.

Beleth looked to his companions, then to the rubbernecked angels, and then back down to the pathetic meat-sack below him and smiled, "You should just end it. You won't be able to go on after he's gone."

Sariel's eyes shot open and he snapped his head down with a new resolve. Adriel had done the same. The Lord had answered their prayers. The two locked eyes, nodded and placed their hands on the hilts of their swords as they stepped forward. The two demons focused on Steven saw the movement and immediately responded in kind. Swords scraped leather and in an instant the two dark beings sat on the edge of Steven's bed like vultures, blades pointed at the approaching angels of light.

The larger one who was completely hairless spoke, "You have no power here. You were ordered. We were told."

Adriel drew his sword and ran it along the side of the demonic steel sending a shower of sparks raining down onto Steven's comforter like a sparkler on the Fourth of July.

"Orders have changed."

"Sariel drew his mammoth sword and held it aloft, "You were simply told what you needed to hear to carry out The Lord's plan. You were nothing but a means to an end."

Beleth shot a hissing glare of pure hatred toward the sound of Sariel's voice. "Keep them away until I'm done!" he barked.

Without an acknowledgement the two leapt from their perch on the bed into the air and descended on the angels like a pair of possessed blenders in a blur of rage filled hacks. Sariel dodged and deflected faster than any human eye could track. A high heavy blow came crashing down with the demon's full weight sending them both to the ground. With the edge of the rusty sword inches from his throat, Sariel cried out, "I will always be with you. Believe!"

Beleth reared back and roared in anger, "Keep them quiet! End them!" He looked back at Conner and placed his mouth over his ear, "Believe that you got your baby brother killed!"

Adriel stepped over a low wide swing of the hairless demon's blade and taking the moment of opportunity, surged forward and put the ornate hilt of his sword through the smooth dark forehead of his opponent with one bone crunching movement. As his attacker's body went limp like someone had just stolen their bones, he let the momentum of his blow carry him across the room and into the snarling beast sitting on Sariel's chest.

The two rolled into the nearest wall with a heavy packing thud, and Sariel immediately sat up and shouted toward Conner, "Believe that you did all you could. God is with you."

Conner's hands slid down the sides of his face leaving deep red lines pulsating on his cheeks. He grabbed his chest and blood began to seep through his shirt. Sariel leap to his feet.

Beleth grabbed the sides of the boy's head and screamed dead into the middle of his face, "Kill yourself! You deserve it! You've earned every single bit of..." The last word was lost in a syrupy gurgle. The tip of Sariel's glowing sword appeared at the bottom of Beleth's sternum and then quickly migrated North, cutting the monster in two from roughly the waist up.

His blade caught in the sinew of Beleth's neck and with a violent yank, it popped free along with the demon's head. When line of sight was restored Sariel drew back and with everything he was, opened himself up to be a conduit for The Lord's message, "Believe In Me And I Will Never Leave You!"

Conner threw back his head and inhaled. Sariel flicked the pieces of gore and Beleth off of his blade and looked back to Adriel.

He was rising from the a puddle of what was once demon. "Praise the Lord Almighty." He said matter-of-factly as he wiped his free hand clean of tar colored blood.

"Praise Him indeed," Sariel turned to Conner who was

now feverishly trying to find the words to talk to his Creator and Savior. "The Lord uses all things for His glory. Praise Him indeed."

Ω

Days passed and the two stood silent guard over the brothers. They rejoiced when Conner had reached out for a copy of The Lord's Book and searched it for knowledge. It never ceased to amaze Sariel how the Lord's plan worked so flawlessly. Allowing the demon access drove the boy straight into the arms of his creator. And today, would be an event to remember as well. Adriel smiled and nodded at his brother in approval. Today he was to appear to the boy and was being permitted to perform what the humans called a miracle.

Conner walked to the blinds and looked back at Steven, "Rise and shine Stevie."

With a quick pull of the string the mountains appeared in the distance with the sun just cresting the top spire. Sariel closed his eyes and added the light of The Creator, blinding the boy. Shock and confusion registered in his face before fear took over.

He watched the boy struggle to keep his balance and once try to open his eyes against the light. Adriel placed a hand on Sariel's shoulder.

"It's time," he whispered.

Sariel squared himself, placed a massive hand over Steven's head and shouted, "Let Everything That Has Breath Praise The Lord!" Conner fell backwards into the window and in an instant The Lord's power flowed through Sariel and healed the young boy.

"Believe." A command and plea. Then they were gone.

V. Nicholas Gerasimou

CHAPTER 5

A DEEPER LOSS

V. Nicholas Gerasimou

A DEEPER LOSS

The back door always stuck. At some point every night his arms would be full and the door wouldn't' budge. He hated that. Every time he would take the trash out the back, Conner would have to lower his shoulder and throw his body weight into the dented steel portal to get it to scrape off it's crooked frame. Some nights were easier than others.

Tonight Conner was near fury. The two full boxes of trash in his arms were leaking some type of putrid, foul smelling sludge down his biceps, and the third kick he'd levied against the metal beast hadn't even phased it.

"Unreal!" He hissed to no one. He stepped back and took a moment to collect himself. There was nowhere to set the boxes down and his apron was getting wet. He stared at the logo painted in the middle of the door. *"Mama D's Italian Kitchen"*

He always found it strange that they'd painted a logo on the inside of the door. What good did it do there? If you were reading it, then you were obviously inside the best, and only Italian restaurant in Redlands. It you were inside you knew where you were, and the logo was just redundant. These were the thoughts that rattled around his head at midnight while bussing tables.

These were the thoughts he pondered while brown sludge

rounded the tip of his elbow and soaked into his sleeve. A sudden burst of rage shot from his brain, and down to his right leg like a current would have if he'd licked a live wire. The front kick he blasted into the middle of the rotund smiling caricature of Mama D sent a shock wave up his spine making his teeth click.

The door sent out a high pitched protest as it begrudgingly let go of it's casing and swung outward. Conner wasn't alarmed by the intense sense of accomplishment and smug satisfaction that washed over him as he walked past the defeated door. The door deserved it. How dare it mess with him? It should have known better.

Now, the large foot shaped dent just below Mama D's ample cleavage… that he didn't plan on. He let his eyes linger on it for a moment longer before shrugging it off and making his way to the dumpster.

A hearty heave-ho and the boxes of filth were resting peacefully with their kin. Conner wiped his hands on his apron and took a moment to breathe. It was strange but he liked it out there. The restaurant was a cramped, loud, poorly lit sweat-box that had the same stereotypical tin-can Italian "*Manga*" music blaring on repeat. Encased meats and netted wine jugs hung from the ceiling, and the plastic red and white checkered table cloths made a shrill rustling sound whenever someone even looked them, let alone touched them.

With all that mania swirling around inside, he liked the silence of the alley to periodically clear his head. He leaned against the weathered red brick wall and looked out across the parking lot. His small alley led out into a large central lot that served as parking for Mama D's, a Rite Aid, the dry cleaners and the twenty-four hour gym next door.

He sighed and shifted his gaze upward. The stars were brilliant tonight. They seemed so close. His mind drifted to whoever put them there. A day hadn't passed over the past three months that he hadn't thought about that surreal morning in Steven's hospital room.

He knew what he saw. He knew what he felt. He saw an

angel standing next to Steven's bed. Or he was suffering from some form of delusional schizophrenia. The only problem with the latter was that it couldn't explain Steven's miraculous recovery. Of course, he could be imagining that too. This could all be a drug addled dream he was swimming though as he drooled himself silly in a hospital bed.

"Come on man," Conner shook off the thought like one does a gnat that buzzes into your ear. He rubbed his face and gave himself a reassuring nod. "I'm fine. Not crazy. Fine. People see angels. Happens all the time."

He walked out around the side of the dumpster, let his back hit the wall and slid down to his haunches resting his forearms on his knees. He was chewing on some pretty serious revelations. If he saw an angel, then God was real. There was a God. It was real. He is real. But, if God was real, that meant the devil was real. If the devil is real, then so are demons. If demons were real, one of them could be standing next to him right now.

A chill ran up his spine and all of the hair on the back of his neck stood up. He slowly rolled his head to the right and let his chin fall on his shoulder. An alley cat stared back at him from a few feet away.

"You're not a demon are you?" He asked. The cat yawned and licked itself where only a cat can, and then slowly trotted off.

"Didn't think so," Conner said back. With a few awkward jerks he wall-walked back up to a standing position. He looked at his phone to get the time. He'd been taking the trash out for close to fifteen minutes. Should probably get back. As he turned to head back toward the nuclear silo blast door that was quietly masquerading as an emergency exit, the sharp tinkle of glass shattering on concrete snapped his head back.

He heard shoes scuffing on gravel covered asphalt punctuated with heavy breathing and muffled grunts. He peaked around the corner of the dumpster into the main expanse of the common lot and saw a man being dragged by his foot by a much larger man, as another cheered him on from behind. The man on the ground kicked back up with his free leg, trying to find purchase for his heel in his attacker's groin.

Without thinking, Conner jogged around the corner and into the lot. The man on the ground had workout clothes on which couldn't have been doing the skin on his back any favors as he slid across a vacant parking space. He was in his mid-thirties and in the dim, yellow tinted overhead lights looked to have brownish hair. When he got within about ten feet of the skirmish Conner noticed a young girl squatting down huddled next to the door of a nearby car. Her arms were wrapped around her knees and by the way she was shaking Conner could tell she was crying.

There was a lot of input, and Conner was trying to process it all and come up with a plan of attack.

"Hey," awkwardly fell out of his mouth like a wet towel on a locker-room floor before he could stop it.

Everything stopped. All three turned and focused on the newcomer.

The shorter of the two, the spectator squared up to Conner, "Take off man. There's nothing here you want."

"You're right… but," he ran a hand through his hair. "Two on one just isn't fair. It's not right"

The man on the ground made eye contact with Conner for a moment and motioned to the girl with his head. Conner squinted back and cocked his head in confusion. The man exaggerated the same movement again, then satisfied turned his attention back to his captured appendage.

He then drew back his free leg and without warning violently drove his foot straight forward through the top of the man's knee who had him by the foot. It bent back at an unnatural angle, and there was an audible snap as some of the ligaments holding some very important bones together let go like dry rubber bands.

He stood for moment like a terrified flamingo balancing on one leg while his other hung and flopped from his hip. Shock and pain fought for supremacy on his face before his eyes rolled back and he attempted a trust fall with no spotter. His head cracked the pavement, which sent his friend sprinting over to where the man in the workout clothes was scooting backwards on his elbows and hips.

Anger and profanity were spewing from his mouth in equal amounts as he jumped on the downed man. He landed a shot before Conner could squat down and wrap an arm around his neck. He snaked the other arm up behind his head and locked his hands.

"Stop fighting! Relax and I'll let go!" Conner kept repeating his request but the writhing man in his arms was unfortunately beyond compliance. He kicked and cursed and tried to reach back to claw at anything within reach.

"Okay, but you did this bud." Conner stood and arched his back taking the man's feet off the ground. He slowly applied more pressure to his hold. The more he squeezed, the less gusto the man threw into his struggle. Tighter still and the cursing slipped into wet unintelligible gurgles. Then there was nothing.

Conner let go and the man folded to the ground like a paper doll. The frantic pace of the moment stopped and Conner was left panting surveying the scene.

"Thank you." Came a voice from below.

He suddenly remembered the man on the ground. "You okay?" He asked.

"Yah, I'm alright," he reached up and Conner took his hand helping him to his feet.

"Tell me they're the a-holes and I didn't just help you hobble that girl's," He pointed to the girl, "boyfriend, and choke out his noble buddy."

"No, you're still a good man my friend. You did a good thing," he said as he looked at the two on the ground. He snapped his eyes up to meet Conner's, "My names' Michael."

Conner looked down and saw Michael's hand was extended and he took it, "Conner," he kept shaking, "By the way, did you flunk out of mime school? How was I supposed to know what," he made an exaggerated show of rolling his head around in a stained arc and flicking his eyes up into his skull like he was passing out, "means?"

"I thought it was perfectly clear. I wanted you to check on the girl because I was going to make a move."

Conner hummed a sarcastic reply.

Michael smiled and clasped Conner's shoulder, "Lets go check on her." He said as he motioned behind him with his nose.

The girl had stood and was leaning against the car door. Michael smiled and gave her a meek wave as he approached.

"Are you okay sweetie?" he asked.

The girl nodded and sniffed in a nose full of tears. "Yah, I'm good. Thank you so much."

Conner opened his hands palms up, "What happened?"

Michael turned and pointed across the parking lot toward the gym, "I was working out, finished up, came out to my car and saw," he turned to the girl, "What's your name honey?"

"Sarah," she replied.

"Sarah here getting hassled by those two idiots. I had to help… so I helped the best I could. That's when you showed up."

Conner looked at Sarah, "Hassle you? How hassled were you?"

She looked up at him and then at Michael. He nodded to her as if she needed his approval to speak. When she looked back to Conner her eyes welled up with tears and they coursed down her cheeks in two thin streams.

"I dropped my keys and they asked me if I needed help. I said no but they kept asking and they came over. The tall one picked up my keys and wouldn't give them back and then they started saying that they would give me a ride home," a hitching sob racked her body and it took her a few moments to collect herself. "Then the shorter one touched me. He," She broke off and covered her face with her hands.

Michael put his arm around her and pulled her in, "I saw it all. I had to help."

A controlled anger bubbled up through Conner's soul

into his brain, "Two questions. One," he held up his index finger, "Does he still have your keys? And two," he held up the index finger on his other hand so it looked like he was making a filed goal in a game of paper football, "He… touched you?"

Sarah straightened up and wiped her eyes on her sleeve. "Yes I think he has my keys," she took a deep shaky breath and closed her eyes, "And yes, he touched me…" Her voice broke off so she simply motioned to her chest with a circular spin of an open hand.

Michael pulled her in again, "It's okay sweetie. You're safe."

Conner nodded and shot a fiery hot blast of air out of his nose. He stomped with dangerous purpose over to the man who's left lower leg seemed to be attached to his body by saran wrap, and stepped on his thigh just above the kneecap. He sat up and howled in agony, Conner just leaned over further and added a few more pounds of pressure to his femur.

"Keys," It was a question and a command rolled into one.

"What!? Get off my leg! You're killing me!"

Conner grabbed a handful of his hair and yanked him forward putting even more pressure on his mangled leg, "I just might. Keys. Now."

The man fought back sobs and reached a shaking hand into his jean pocket and produced a set of keys held together by a Hello Kitty doll that had definitely seen better days. Conner let go of his hair and went to make stop two on his brief To-Do list. The shorter man had regained consciousness and was on his hands and knees coughing up saliva and phlegm, that had drained down his throat when Conner turned his brain off.

During his football tenure every player had a secret dream of being able to kick a game winning field goal. Before practice they would all line up and take turns trying to kick that ball through the uprights. It always ended badly and was always entertaining. Conner's problem was that he always tried to kick the ball with everything he was worth. He put all of his momentum and strength into the swing, and that would inevitably send the ball rocketing off at a ridiculous angle far from where he'd intended it to go.

Tonight, Conner was going to try to kick a winner. A sixty yarder to win the game and make him a legend. He stomped up directly behind the wheezing would-be rapist and drew back his right leg as far as it would go.

"*Keep your head down.*" That's what his buddy Mike, their kicker would always yell at him at the last minute before he swung. Conner kept his head down. Toe pointed. Arms relaxed and fluid. He brought his foot up into the man's groin with such force it lifted him off the ground and sent him rolling into the curb a few feet away.

"Conner," Michael's voice snapped him out of his trance. "I think they get the point. They've more than enough paid for what they've done tonight. Let The Lord handle them."

The mention of God deflated any bravado left out of Conner's anger balloon. His shoulders slumped, he nodded and walked back to Michael and Sarah.

"Sorry about that. I got a little upset," he said with a shrug.

"A little?" Michael said, peeking around Conner at the two writhing men.

"Okay. More than a little."

Sarah smiled and a nervous giggle popped out of her mouth, "I didn't mind. Thank you."

Conner breathed out a soft laugh and handed her back her keys, "You okay to get home? We could follow you."

"No, I'll be alright. Thank you two so much. My guardian angels." She reached up and hugged them both.

"You have no idea," Conner mumbled into the top of her head.

Ω

The business card sat on top of his desk, a few feet from his face. He studied it like it was a new species of animal. He would pick it up, turn it in his hands, look at the name and then gently put it back down.

"Michael Hill," Conner said out loud to nobody. Michael... Hill," he chewed on each syllable like he was learning a new language. Michael had handed it to him last night before they parted ways. He said he had wanted to talk. When Conner asked about what, he had pointed to the sky, then straight into Conner's chest. So it was either about his relationship with God, or a very slow disco dance-craze that was about to sweep the nation. He had his money on the first option.

It was just that the thought of calling a grown man, whom he had met last night, under interesting circumstances in a back parking lot, and spoken to for no more than five minutes, unnerved him a little. For lack of more eloquent phrasing; it just made him feel weird. The only reason he was even flirting with the idea of picking up the phone was that his card claimed that Michael was the lead pastor for the Mission Life Church of San Bernardino.

That actually wasn't entirely true; Conner also just sensed something about the man. It was a warm genuine quality and a sense of peace that simply radiated off of him like a pleasant cologne. Conner caught himself smirking as he thought about it which made him even more self conscious and awkward.

The final nail in the coffin, was what Michael had said before they left. Conner slapped him on the shoulder and said, "Sure was lucky I took the trash out when I did," mostly because he couldn't think of anything else to say and the silence was painful.

Michael immediately came back with, "Oh I don't believe in coincidence. It was no mistake that you came out here tonight when you did. I believe the Lord led you here, at that exact time, for a specific purpose."

Conner looked like a child who had just been told he was about to learn where Santa Clause, the Easter Bunny and the Tooth Fairy hung out on the weekends. "What's that?"

"I don't know," Michael said, "To keep me from getting my teeth kicked in?" Michael watched Conner deflate in disappointment. "Look, I'm getting a feeling that it would be a good thing if you and I talked for a bit. It's kind of a part of my job." That's when he handed Conner the card, and that in turn led to the cardstock dilemma taunting Conner from his desktop.

Ω

Since that day in the hospital room, Conner had seen the world differently. He tried to look behind the curtain that he was positive was hanging just in front of his eyes. He looked for signs everywhere. Angels, demons, fairies, unicorns… you name it. He wanted to tell someone. Unfortunately, he didn't know how to share what he'd seen, and what he knew, in a way that would make any sense. Not the kind of sense he wanted it to make.

He just wanted to be able to turn to his neighbor and say, "Oh my gosh! Did you see that?" And have them say right back, "I sure did bud. I'm right there with you, and you're not insane or a danger to yourself or others, and you defiantly shouldn't be heavily medicated and under close professional supervision." That's what he wanted.

And as crazy as it sounded, when he said it out loud, he thought he may have found that person in Michael. Someone who could give him validation, and answers at the same time. It was worth it.

Each ring seeped another microgram of adrenaline into Conner's veins. This was torturous. Didn't this guy set up voicemail on his phone? It's rung like a hundred times, or three, but who's counting? Conner was praying it would go to voicemail, or his battery would die, or maybe even if his phone exploded in his hand it would alleviate the growing tension that was twisting up his guts like a ball of yarn.

Just as he was about to hit the end button with his thumb, satisfied that he had given it his honest effort and apparently God didn't want him to talk; he heard Michael's voice coming out of the earpiece, "Hello?"

Conner was struck dumb by shock. He stood with his mouth open for a full two-count before his brain rebooted, "Hi, Michael. This is Michael right? This is Conner. From last night, in the parking lot. You gave me your card, so I'm calling you. Yup."

"Conner, I was hoping you would call. I've been praying for you." Came Michael's calm reply.

Conner paused because he wasn't quite sure what the appropriate response was to that statement. "Thanks?" He closed his eyes and shook his head in embarrassed frustration. He continued, "I know you said you wanted to sit down and talk about… things. So, I'm open to chatting."

Conner's discomfort was almost palpable so Michael tried to put him at ease, "Conner did you read my card?"

Conner picked it up and held it in at eye level, "Yes. I read it."

"Then you know what it is I do. What the Lord has called me to do." Michael said. "I do my best to spread the word of Jesus Christ. In any circumstance I find myself in. Even in confrontations in back alleys."

"It's really more of a parking lot," Conner immediately kicked himself.

Michael smiled, "Agreed. Regardless, with the providence of last night I truly felt The Lord pushing me toward you. It was no accident."

"Okay. What do you want to talk about?" Conner asked.

"I have no idea, I know this may seem strange to you but there is no pressure here. We can simply get a cup of coffee and talk about nothing if you want, and if you have questions for me I'd be happy to do my best to answer them."

Conner mulled the proposition of having an awkward cup of coffee with a grown man for a moment, then nodded approvingly at his bookshelf, "Okay sure. When do you want to meet?"

"Well," Michael said, "What are you doing right now?"

Ω

Conner arrived early and found a table outside, away from any prying eyes or ears. He wasn't sure why he felt so self-conscious, but it was driving him crazy. He sat at the small metal table and nervously played chess with the napkin holder and sugar packets as he waited. Cursory glances at the sidewalk traffic took his mind off of his nervous hand for a moment. The people looked so content. They walked by with small smiles playing on their mouths, having laughter filled, animated conversations on their phones and taunting Conner with how well they seemed to have it all figured out.

He wondered if under the smiles and small talk they had some of the same questions gnawing on them that were eating him alive. Didn't they know what was going on all around them? Didn't they care? A high pitched screech brought him back to the moment. He saw Michael parking his blue pickup across the street. It sounded like he needed to check his brakes; he could be chewing up his rotors.

His car door slammed shut and Michael jogged across the street. He didn't look weird. Blue jeans, a tee-shirt, shaggy brown hair; he just kind of looked like… a guy.

Ω

"Hey! Good to see you," Michael said as he extended his hand, in the other was a worn Bible.

"You too," Conner replied.

"You been waiting long?" He let go and sat down next to Conner.

"No I got here about ten minutes ago. I wanted to be sure we got as table."

Michael took a look behind him at the ghost town of a coffee shop they were outside of. The Baristas were inside throwing coffee beans into empty cups across the counter to keep themselves awake.

"Good thing you did. This place is jumpin." He turned back around smiling.

There was a moment of very awkward silence so Michael broke it. "Okay, I'm going to go give those kids in there something to do and get us some coffee," he got up and walked around the table, "Do something for me. While I'm gone I want you to read something." He flipped open the Bible and thumbed to the book of Proverbs. The pages made a light breathy sound as he turned them. It was soothing.

"Read this chapter," he stuck his finger at the top of sixteen, "and when I come back with our java I want to talk to you about it."

Conner looked and quickly scanned the page, then looked up at Michael, "Alright."

Proverbs sixteen; he began to read. They mostly sounded like antic-dotes. Stuff like "Never look a gift horse in the mouth," and "A bird in the hand is worth two in the bush." Line after line he breezed through the chapter, rolling his eyes at the antiquated little pearls of wisdom. That is until he got verse nine.

He read it and it was like someone hit the emergency brake on his eyes. He re-read it again and again.

Ω

"I hope you like heavy cream and two sugars in your coffee. I kind of took the liberty of fixing them both up for us. Hope you don't mind." Michael set Conner's cup down next to him and sat back into his chair. He took a small sip of his own and crossed his legs, "Well, what did you think?"

Conner put his hand to his mouth and thought for a moment and then pointed to a line in the middle of the page.

"This line. This line right here."

Michael leaned forward and spun the Bible around to see where Conner had his finger pegged. It was pressing into verse nine.

"Good verse. Catchy. It's actually one of my favorites," he said with a smile. He took a long sip, swallowed and recited it, "In his heart a man plans his course, but The Lord determines his steps."

Conner stared down into his steaming cup and took a deep burdened breath. "So what does it all mean?" He looked up into Michael's eyes, "How does it work?"

A chuckle danced up Michael's throat and leap out his mouth, "How does what work bud?"

Conner let a frustrated shrug answer for him. When it earned a blank expectant stare back in return he started to count off his spiritual checklist on his fingers, "God. Jesus. Angels. Demons. Salvation. The Plan."

Michael sat forward, set his cup down and steepled his fingers, "Conner… that is two years of study in seminary school to merely scratch the surface. What I can tell you is that God is real, He knows who you are and He has a plan for you."

"Oh I know He's real. That I have no doubt of."

"Really? Would you mind telling me why?" Michael asked.

Conner threw up his hands in a show of surrender, "Sure, why not."

So Conner told him about everything that had gone on the past year. He recanted the magic bullet and the amazingly vivid dream that shook him to his core. He shared about his attempt to do a live-action thematic reenactment of Roadhouse in a dirty bar in the high desert. He fought back a few tears when he spoke about how he almost lost his brother and he paused when he got to his miraculous recovery.

"Then there was someone in the room with us. I went blind and then there was someone in the room."

Michael nodded and motioned for Conner to continue. "So, I'm standing there blind from… from something, and then I hear someone move by Steven's bed. I really tried to open my eyes and for a second I saw like an outline of a person."

"Who? Nurse? Doctor?" Michael asked with calm

sincerity.

"No. And I think you know where I'm going with this." Conner said as he rubbed his forehead.

Michael put a reassuring hand on Conner's forearm, "There is no judgment here. I'm here to listen. Just tell me what happened."

He nodded and took a deep breath, "Okay, so I see this… person and try to get an answer. A few seconds go by and then it was like someone stuck my head in a woofer and kicked the gain up to ten. I hear the person in the room say *Let Everything That Has Breath Praise The Lord*. It was unreal."

"Then what?"

"The guy's voice lowers to normal and he tells me to believe, then he's gone. The next second my little brother is talking to me."

"Just like that?" Asked Michael.

"Just like that," Conner replied. "I'm not being dramatic. I'm not a crazy person, or the guy who sees bigfoot in his backyard or Jesus' face burned into a slice of toast."

Michael smiled, "Just say it."

Conner leveled his gaze and locked eyes with Michael, "I saw an angel. A real angel. He was in my brother's hospital room and he talked to me, and then magically healed my little brother's brain with his big crazy angel hands. Happy?"

"Big crazy angel hands?"

"That's what you're focusing on?" Conner snipped back.

Michael shot a laugh out his nose, "I believe you."

"You believe me." Conner parroted.

"Yes. I believe you. I believe that you were visited by a messenger of God and that messenger preformed a miracle and healed your little brother. What did you say his name was?"

"Steven."

"Yah, Steven. Conner, God isn't a theory or a happy idea. He's as real as this cup of coffee," Michael picked it up and thoughtfully turned it in his hand, "He is real Conner. Right here, right now. He isn't a story."

Conner sat quiet for a few moments chewing on what Michael had said. He opened his mouth to say something but snapped it shut and swallowed the sentence whole. He knew what he wanted to say but his brain stingily refused to share the revelation with his vocal cords. The struggle flashed across his face in waves.

Conner finally nodded and locked eyes with Michael, "I know. I know that's how I should feel. I do. But I look around here," he motioned to the street with a grand sweep of his arm, "And it all seems so surreal, so far away. Why can't I just believe? What if I hallucinated it? What if I'm crazy?"

A tear snuck out of his eye, slid an erratic path down his cheek and quietly disappeared into the corner of his mouth. "What is wrong with me?" He leaned in closer to Michael, "I'm ninety-nine percent sure I saw an angel and he magically healed my brother's brain and I'm still having trouble buying in. Does that make me a bad person?"

Michael sighed and put and hand on Conner's shoulder, "Conner listen to me. The Bible is full of stories of people not believing in God and we just take them for granted. Moses led Israel out of Egypt and they saw countless miracles of the Lord working in their lives," he slapped the table making Conner jump, "They still didn't believe and many of them rejected him." He sat back and held his hands about two feet apart, "God parted the Red Sea for them. Can you imagine seeing that? They were still disobedient. A pillar of magical fire led them at night and clouds during the day. Bread fell from the sky and water came out of rocks to quench their thirst and still, no dice. Can you imagine walking with Jesus? How incredible. But there were people who stood next to Him, shoulder to shoulder, watched Him perform miracles with their own eyes and still had disbelief."

Conner shook his head. "That's nuts."

"Well they did. They refused to believe the truth that was right in front of them," he reached out and grabbed Conner's arm, "Conner, last night when I saw those two men attacking that defenseless little girl, I didn't even question whether or not

The Lord was with me. I knew He was, and I knew that I was doing what He wanted me to do."

"How? How did you know?"

Michael smiled, "I heard Him. In my soul, in my head. He told me to go. Do you think it was chance that you came out back right when you did? Do you think we met by accident? Do you think that random coincidence landed you here, talking to me about the thing that we're talking about?" Michael thumped his finger on the cover of the Bible, "In his heart a man plans his course, but The Lord determines his steps. He has a plan for you Conner. From the beginning He had you in mind."

Conner rubbed the back of his neck with both hands in a show of frustration, "In mind for what?"

Michael chomped on the end of each word for effect, "I. Don't. Know."

"Thanks."

"Look, you're here. He's finally got your attention. Now you're looking for the signs. You're on the path bud."

Ω

Conner and Michael spoke for close to three more hours that afternoon. Conner shared every deep dark doubt and question he had about God and to his amazement Michael seemed to have a perfect Bible verse, and a way to relate it to his life that made perfect sense. When they felt they had talked enough for one day, Michael invited Conner to attend one of his church services that coming Sunday.

"I really think you'll enjoy it." He said.

"Sure, sounds good." Conner agreed.

When they reached his faded blue sedan Michael stopped and faced Conner. "There's one more thing that I would like to ask if you don't mind."

"What's on your mind?"

"I'd like to pray with you."

Conner made a show of looking around the street with raised eyebrows, "Here?"

"Yes. Here," Michael replied.

"Right... *here.*" Conner repeated while pointing to the little piece of street he was currently a resident of.

Michael smiled, "Yes, I feel moved to pray with you right now. I promise I won't make a scene."

The voice in his head kept telling him to feel embarrassed and ashamed about what he was about to do, but Michael's confidence and quiet faith kept them at bay long enough for Conner to agree. Michael bowed his head and discreetly took Conner's hand.

"Lord, thank you for bringing Conner and I together today. I pray that you help him to accept your love and believe in the unconditional nature of it. Please let today be the day that he fully comes to you, without any reservations. He's made the hardest step... the first one."

At first, Conner was acutely aware of the fact that he was holding hands with a grown man in the middle of the street, in the middle of the day. He could feel the eyes of every passerby boring into him like a drill-bit, angrily chewing through a two-by-four. They were judging him, ridiculing the both of them. Then something strange happened; the only reason it was strange was the fact that it was so simple.

Conner just started listening to what Michael was saying. The world disappeared and Conner became lost in his words. It was the honest, genuine emotion with which Michael was praying for him with; deep down he wanted to accept and believe it all, he just wasn't sure how.

"Lord, I know that in coming to you one must suffer a loss of sorts. A servant must lost their pride and independence. To accept you is to reject evil; but a deeper loss is suffered if one chooses not to accept your love. A loss so great it can't be measured. The loss brings in the darkness of being separated from you and Conner has tasted a small hint of what that might be like. I pray for him Lord. I pray that he opens up his heart, mind and soul to you. I pray that you work in his life and carry his load, because his is too heavy for him to carry alone anymore. Please help him admit it."

He looked up at Conner, "We can do nothing good except through Him. He loves you unconditionally, no matter what you do. If you believe in Him He will never leave or forsake you."

Conner exhaled like someone had put a fist through his ribcage and emotion washed over him. The lock that had been spot-welded onto the door to Conner's soul broke. Tears welled in his eyes and began to flow down his cheeks. The man who had been self-conscious about praying in public just a few moments earlier, was now openly crying for the world to see.

"Everything you're ever done in your life has led you to this moment to be here, right now for this purpose. All you have to do ask," said Michael.

"I want him in my life," Conner whispered.

"He's already here," Michael said as he put a hand on his shoulder.

V. Nicholas Gerasimou

CHAPTER 6

A DEEPER LOSS: BEHIND THE VEIL

V. Nicholas Gerasimou

A DEEPER LOSS: BEHIND THE VEIL

Beer dribbled down his chin and soaked the collar of his shirt. He absently wiped at it with the back of his free hand. That was it. Twelve pack gone and they were out of cash. Mark forced a sharp belch out of his throat and reveled in the echo it made in the parking lot. He looked through the window of the car he was leaning against to see if the door was unlocked, or if a window was cracked a little too much.

"Any luck?" he called over to Julian.

"No man. These people have trust issues," they both laughed at that. Julian stooped by a side mirror, checked his teeth and fixed his greasy black hair. The two had been checking cars for the past two hours, and so far they'd scored five iPods, and two wallets with about twenty dollars total in them. They'd used the cash to buy the twelve pack of beer. Mark found a laptop computer that some idiot had tried to hide under the passenger side seat.

So far, not bad but they needed more cash to get the two eight-balls they wanted for later. Car after car they worked their way up and down the isles.

As the two men lurked between the cars, several dark beings tittered around above them leaping from roof to roof,

137

hood to hood. They reeked of hate and sulfur. Every few minutes one would jump down and whisper in Mark's ear, another in Julian's. The men were soaked to the core in sin. They relished it.

Julian waved Mark over near to where he was standing. Mark bumped him with his shoulder, "What's up?"

Julian pointed across the lot at a young girl walking toward them. Her head was down as she awkwardly fumbled in her purse for her keys.

"Looks like our night just got a bit more interesting," Mark said through an evil smile.

Julian's eyes widened with curiosity then quickly narrowed with evil intent, "You got a weapon?"

Mark shook his head, "Nah we don't need one. Sides I don't want to rob her, I want *her*. Look at that body."

A wraith had climbed up onto his back like a tumor and was feeding sick, depraved, lustful thoughts into his mind. He welcomed them.

"This is gonna be good," Julian quipped and he walked over toward where she was headed. A finger twitter, a momentary loss of concentration and the young girl's keys flipped from her hand and tinkled to the ground. Julian was on them like a cat on a mouse. He dropped to a knee and palmed the keys with the worn Hello Kitty hanging from the side.

"You okay?" he asked.

Sarah jumped back and put her hands to her mouth, "Oh, yes I'm fine."

"Sorry I didn't mean to startle you little miss. You just look like you could use some help," Julian said as Mark walked up behind her.

From behind her right shoulder came Mark's voice, "We'll give you a ride home."

Adrenaline poured into Sarah's veins and she started to play out the possible scenarios of her night in her head at breakneck speed. None of them ended with her in one piece.

"No please. I'm okay. Can I have my keys so I can leave?" She asked.

Mark leaned in and took a deep lungful of her hair. She smelled like lavender. "Listen we're going to give you a ride home and you're not going to scream or something very violent might happen."

Julian reached out and took a generous handful of Sarah's chest in his hand and kneaded it like dough. A cry escaped her lips and Mark clamped an iron grip down on her upper arm making her wince. Behind him, the dark creature looking over his shoulder unfurled two black leathery wings from it's back and smiled.

This was perfect. Dagon motioned to a few of his companions and they gathered around the three like they were watching a movie.

They were so enthralled with the show that none of them noticed the man walk around the corner into the lot. None of them noticed his mammoth winged shadow. They were all too busy barking sick encouragement to the two depraved men, to hear an angelic blade the length of a garden rake unsheathe and hum through the air. Nor the sound of the man's footfalls scraping like sandpaper against the gravel on the asphalt.

The demon to Dagon's left cleaved in half from the crown of his head to the worn animal skin belt clasped around his waist. It was if someone had instantly peeled an evil banana. The remaining demons shrieked and scattered into the air like crows just as Michael's hand shot out and grabbed a solid fistful of Mark's hair. With a powerful yank Mark was on his heals and falling backwards. Michael's protector leapt into the air and hung directly over him swinging his blade in a wide arc.

Julian recoiled and Michael took the opportunity to charge, tackling him at the waist. Sarah slid down against the side of the car and fought the sobs that were forcing their way out of her throat.

Mark quickly recovered and jumped onto Michael's back slipping an arm around his neck pulling him up so Julian could scoot out from underneath.

Above them, Michael's protector Hamon was busy

fending off half-a-dozen rage filled spirits with Dagon as the tip of the spear.

With a powerful thrust of his legs, Michael pushed back against Mark and heaved them both backward onto the pavement. Julian got his feet under him and quickly made his way over to them. He steadied himself and started leveling violent, but ill-aimed kicks at his attacker's mid-section. A few of them accidentally found purchase in Mark's ribcage easing his grip on Michael's neck.

Mark let go and rolled away leaving Julian standing over Michael trying to tap-dance his foot through his stomach. He reached down and grabbed Michael's heel to stop him from squirming.

No more than sixty seconds had passed when Sariel decided to announce his presence. He had been watching the ordeal from atop a brick retaining wall next to Mama D's. Conner had just decided to investigate the skirmish and had started to make his way into the lot, when Sariel let his Glory shine forth like the sun, illuminating the entire lot. This understandably caught the attention of all of the heavenly beings present. Conner drew the attention of the rest.

Sariel leapt into the air as Michael put his heel through Julian's knee. He shouldered up to Hamon, and began to slash through the cloud of demons that hung over the skirmish like a dreary morning in June. When Conner made his move to keep Mark from turning Michael's face into oatmeal, the guardians were well into their routine.

Shrieks and curses flew at the two hovering warriors, they sent angelic steel back. Sariel placed his sword on his shoulder, placed both of his massive hands on the hilt and swung like he was trying to hit a game winning grand-slam in the bottom of the ninth. The snake-like wraith descending on him from above popped like an over-inflated water balloon. The tattered demonic remains drew back and rallied behind Dagon.

Below them, Conner had just helped Michael to his feet. Sariel opened his arms and addressed the dark group, "This meeting was ordained by the Most High. It was meant to be.

You have no power here. You may stay if you wish, and perish. Or flee and continue your sinful existence. The choice is yours. It is of no consequence to me."

Hamon drew a second shorter blade from his belt and clashed the two together sending a shower of sparks floating to the ground, "I sincerely hope you all decide to stay. I was just beginning to warm up and enjoy myself."

Sariel shot him a sideways glance and a smile momentarily flashed across his face. Dagon hissed at the two glowing beings and then vanished into the darkness quickly followed by the last few stragglers.

The two angels watched with a detached curiosity as Conner planted his foot in the man's groin sending him rolling into the curb. Hamon slowly looked to Sariel and grunted with approval.

Sariel closed his eyes and sighed, "The spirit is in him, but he is still searching. Still lost."

Hamon lightly rested a hand on his shoulder, "He is one of God's chosen, and this..." he motioned to the two men speaking below them with a short sweep of his arm, "...is a meeting The Lord has had planned for quite a while. It will put him on the path."

Sariel nodded, "He has shared a small part of The Plan with me. I only know what I know, and this meeting will send my charge toward a glorious purpose that The Most High needs him to accomplish."

"Praise be to God!" Hamon yelled with authority.

"Praise be to God indeed!"

V. Nicholas Gerasimou

CHAPTER 7

GLORY IN THE STREET

V. Nicholas Gerasimou

GLORY IN THE STREET

Sometimes the little things in life are what mean the most. They are also the easiest to overlook. Conner let his head fall back and he filled his lungs with the crisp morning air. He shut his eyes and took another chest bulging breath. He loved that smell. There was something about the way that wet asphalt mixed with a cold morning breeze that just made him think of home. He couldn't explain it.

The sun had crested the Santa Ana Mountain range to the East, and flooded the coastal valley with a soft warmth. It was going to be a beautiful day.

"Thank you Lord," Conner whispered under his breath. He absently rubbed the small metal cross that now hung around his neck. As he dropped his hand away, his index finger grazed the top of a thick scar that sprang from his collarbone and ran down his chest.

Vivid images of a horrible day looped in his mind momentarily ripping him away from his perfect morning. The horrible emotions that were married to that day in the desert made a second volley, and attempted to break through his calm. Conner shook them away and flippantly ran his fingers through his hair.

He was here and he was thankful for it. Months ago he

stood in the middle of a not-so-busy street and prayed for salvation. He prayed for peace. He prayed for direction. He prayed that no one would notice him holding hands with a grown man in the middle of the day. The Lord saw fit to answer every single request.

The lock made of fear and doubt that had been molded over Conner's heart broke that day. In the weeks that followed he was a man sized exposed nerve. He felt everything. Like the dentist had just decided to wing-it with no Novocain and a dull drill. Regret, remorse, guilt, disgust, fear; they washed over him like the tide, in waves. But beneath it all was love. A love he had never felt before. That's what made it bearable.

When he was alone in his room, and the weight of the way he had lived his life was sitting on his chest making it hard to breathe, and the realization of how much time he had wasted started to fill his mind with sorrow, that love would come rushing in like a river that had breached a levy. As hokey as it sounded that was the only way he could describe it. It was like he was covered in filth and when it became unbearable he was simply washed clean.

Conner devoured the Bible. He became a regular at Michael's church. He became the person he used to scoff at who would talk to strangers about Jesus and pray before meals in public. It all made sense to him now.

Ω

The line outside to get in the door, to get into the Starbucks, to wait in the line to order his Venti-Half-Caff-Caramel-Macchiatto, snaked past the double-wide bay-window with the green mermaid, and continued to grow past the adjacent dry cleaners as throngs of foggy eyed caffeine deprived zombies dragged themselves into place to get their fix. Conner nudged Steven forward with a raised shoulder when the line moved.

"Put your phone away," he sighed at his brother.

Steven smirked and shoved it in his pocket, "So are you going to guilt trip me if I don't go?"

Conner held out his hands like he was expecting a hug, "Why wouldn't you go? What's the big deal? It's one night of your life."

"So if I don't go, then I'm a bad person?" Steven asked.

Conner shook his head, "No. You're not a bad person. I just want you to *want* to go… and you should *want* to go." He nodded with satisfaction, confident that he'd made his point.

The line crawled forward a few feet and the brothers paused their debate long enough to shuffle toward the door.

"Church?" The word flopped out of Steven's mouth like a dead fish.

Conner's face softened, "Steven, it's not going to be like you're thinking. God doesn't live in a shiny white building and He's not an angry old man who's judging you. He loves you."

"It's not God that bugs me. It's the," he raised his hands to the sky and shook them like tambourines, "church people." He dropped into a very Foghorn-Leghorn-esk, Looney Tunes caricature of a slimy southern preacher, "I say, I say, I say… praise Je-sus ya'll!"

His hand shot out like a piston and Steven slapped his palm against Conner's forehead. Conner didn't react, but simply let his eyes slowly track up to his brother's wrist. "You are-ah Heeeaaaled-ah!" With that he shoved Conner backward and clapped. "Now-ah, send me your money and Gawd will bless-ah you."

From somewhere behind them someone threw a very annoyed sounding cough their direction. Conner looked up and noticed a small gulf had developed between them, and the woman who was waiting in front of them with her small daughter. The little girl was spinning at a dizzying pace around her mother's knees. The knitted woolen tassels that dangled from her coat were spun out so that they looked like streamers. Conner stared for a moment with a furrowed brow because she reminded him of something. He couldn't quite find the word. He hated that.

They were breaking the accepted line-waiting etiquette by not instantly closing the gap. Raised eyebrows and a flick of the head informed Steven of their transgression. They were close enough now that when the door opened a warm breeze filled with chocolate and cinnamon teasingly hugged them for a few moments before being cruelly strangled by the frigid air outside.

"Whirling Dervish!" he exclaimed with a snap of his fingers like he'd just blown Alec Trebec's mind by crushing the Final Jeopardy question.

"Huh?" Steven said with a sideways look.

"Those guys who spin around in airports in the robes. Whirling Dervish. That's what she looked like." Conner explained.

"Who?" Steven asked, searching the line with wide eyes for effect.

"The little girl. She was... never-mind."

He shook his head and pinched the bridge of his nose to regain his train of thought, "Anyway... church.. It's not like that. Look, I get it. I know why you feel weird, but the people at this church are just normal people. They're... like me." Conner said as he thumbed his chest.

A sideways smile curved the corner of Steven's mouth, "Normal? Like you? Then I'm defiantly not going."

"Shut up." Conner said with a shove that moved Steven to the door. "Go. Get me my usual, I'll grab a table out here."

"Okay." Steven said with a small salute.

Ω

Conner huffed out a dragon tendril of misty breath into the cold morning air. The street was starting to wake up. It was like it was a living thing. As the sunlight painted the walls and storefronts a dawn tinted orange, the activity level picked up akin to what happens when you poke an anthill with a stick.

Cars started to whizz by the faded crosswalk Conner was

parked in front of. His table was centered in the deepest part of the trench pressed into the sidewalk that marked the entrance to his side of the street. Conner acted as the unofficial greeter to each new conqueror of the asphalt sea. A few seconds of uncomfortable eye contact and a nod sent each traveler on their merry way.

Blinds unfurled, *Open* signs blinked to life and the chatter of movement blended together to create a symphony of the mundane that melted into the background of simply being outside.

"Here," Conner jumped at the sound of his brother's voice. He turned in his seat and craned his neck. Steven was standing behind him with a steaming cup of coffee in each hand.

"Here!" He said it again wrapped in urgency. He accentuated the command by hitting Conner in the shoulder with the cup that belonged to him.

"Seriously I'm going to pour this in your face. They ran out of the cardboard sleevy things. It's cooking my palm!"

Conner smirked and with a ginger hand, guided his cup of caffeine laced milk and sugar down to the table. He scooted his chair around to face Steven as he plopped down in the adjacent chair.

Steven's faced dropped. He fired an angry glare down toward his crotch, sighed and then snapped his eyes back up to meet his brother's. "Seat is soaked with dew."

Conner let a lazy half-hearted laugh slip out, "Yah, hey… the seats are wet. You should wipe them off before you sit down."

"Thanks," Steven shot back with some venom as he took a sip of his brew.

Conner smiled back over the top of his cup and tentatively tested the waters of his drink with the tip of his tongue.

"Diss isth hoth," Conner slobbered with his tongue dangling out of his mouth.

Steven smirked, "Told you. Can't say you don't deserve

it."

Ω

The world was perfect... and pretty... and pink. Everyone should have a puppy and a bunny, and people were nice and funny and everyone liked saying hello. At least that's was how Maribelle saw the world.

It was cold outside and her Mommy made her put on a coat before they left the house. She wanted to wear the shiny purple raincoat with the unicorn on the back. Her Mommy said it wasn't raining and that she should wear her furry one with the fluffy balls hanging off the collar. That was okay because she liked the way they danced around her neck when she twirled... and she loved to twirl. Her Mommy said she was the best twirler she'd ever seen.

The coffee shop was fun because Mommy always let her get a treat. Today she was leaning toward the chocolate chip muffin that almost seemed to be waving to her from inside the glass case. As she twirled around her mother's legs the man standing behind them caught her eye. He looked lonely.

"He-llo," she sang to him.

"Hi sweety," Steven said back with a flutter of his fingers.

Her mother turned around and smiled, Steven returned it. They were almost to the register.

"Belly, let's go sweetie," her mother said. Maribelle gave the nice man the biggest smile she could muster, all teeth and gums, eyes squeezed shut.

"She's a cutie," Steven said to her mother as he smiled back.

"Thanks. She makes my job a lot easier when she's like this," she reached down and brushed a strand of brown hair out of her face, "Which is pretty much all the time."

Ω

The transmission kept grinding. It sounded like he'd put an entire silverware drawer in a blender and hit puree. It was ridiculous that his dispatcher kept sending him out in this death-trap. Jesse hated it. It never stayed in gear, if he could get it there at all. The driver's side door was stuck so he had to get in and out of the bay doors at the back of the van.

Springs poked through the seat and would inevitably find their sharp piercing way into his rear at inopportune moments and there was the ventilation problem. He was pretty sure at some point they would find him slumped over the steering wheel after missing three revolutions at an intersection stop light.

His cloudy lifeless eyes would be staring straight ahead into the void. The dirty green hat with the United Parcel Delivery patch that had started to fray and roll off, would be up on the dash from when his head bumped the steering wheel. And it would all be because his cheap, lazy dispatcher refused to tell the fat, worthless garage manager that delivery van number seven had a cracked seal from the engine housing, and was pumping enough carbon monoxide exhaust into the cab to choke an elephant.

So it was in Jesse's life. Little pebbles of frustration kept dropping into his glass of tolerance and they were dangerously close to spilling over. He had to drive with his head partially hanging out of the open window like a dog. A window that never fully sealed when rolled up, which made deliveries on days that it rained a joy.

The van rocked to a stop and Jesse slapped the clipboard down on his lap and began to check his list of stops for the day. Six boxes of paper to the postal annex, flowers to some lady named Sarah who worked at the bridal boutique two doors down from there, and three packages full of documents of some kind for the notary next to the drycleaners. He hated this job.

Steam boiled off the lip of the cup like dry ice out of a plastic witches caldron at Halloween. Conner held it in front of his face and inhaled.

"Stevie," Conner said, "Jesus is more than church. He's more than religion. He's more than people singing and raising their hands in the air like they just don't care."

Steven shot a finger pistol at his brother's chest, "Yah, that always kind of freaked me out. It's like they're in some kind of creepy zombie trance. Then they start seizing and spouting gibberish, and then they are healed-ah."

Conner sighed and nodded, "I know. It can look really bad, depending on who you look at. But all I'm asking you to do, is come with me and look at it from a different perspective. My perspective," he said as softly placed his open palm over his chest.

He set down his cup and scooted forward in his chair. "God is real little brother. He exists."

Steven thoughtfully puckered his lips and tilted his head to the side like a dog, "I know. I mean… I believe in God. Something's got to be up there," he said as he flicked a finger skyward.

"That's good, I'm glad. But understand that God isn't some old man with a white beard, who sits on a cloud playing a harp all day. He's real," Conner turned his head and pointed at a delivery man across the street wrestling with a hand-truck stacked neck high with boxes, "He's as real as him… you… as real as me. And He loves you."

A smile spread across Steven's face as his eyes shot behind Conner's right shoulder. He fluttered his fingers in front of his nose.

"Hell-oo," Maribelle chirped back through a chocolate smeared grin.

"Hi sweetie. I see your Mommy got you your muffin," Steven said with wide welcoming eyes.

Maribelle's gaze snapped to the mangled remnants of the once proud chocolate treat gripped in her left hand. Surprise and joy registered on her face as if she were seeing it for the first time, "Yes!"

Conner turned in his seat and saw a caricature of cuteness wearing a woolen coat with tassels dangling from the collar. The little girl simply beamed with happy. He tracked up to her mother. The twirling ball of joy standing behind his chair was definitely her mother's daughter. Same blue eyes, slender nose and sandy brown hair, just around three decades behind.

"She's a doll," Conner said with a smile.

"Thanks, she's my little mini-me. Huh Belly?" She said as she ran a hand through her daughter's hair.

"Mini-me!" Maribelle parroted back with a giggle. That kicked off a new round of twirling as she sang her alliterative new title, "Mini-me, mini-me, mini-me…"

Conner and Steven laughed and Maribelle's mother reached into her purse to fish for her keys, "Okay honey, say bye-bye to the nice men. We're going home."

The tornado of tassels jerked to a stop and Maribelle fixed her gaze on the brothers, "Okay, bye." With that she turned to the crosswalk and took a giant deliberate step toward the painted yellow lines. Her mother grabbed her hand, quickly scanned the street and they headed out.

Ω

Just an ordinary Tuesday morning. The sun rose in the East, and barring a cosmic disaster it would set in the Pacific Ocean just behind Catalina Island later that evening. Plans were made, routines were kept and the world spun on.
Conner turned his head back to Steven and to the conversation they kept hop-scotching through.

"She was cute," he said in between sips.

"Which one?" Steven asked with raised eyebrows.

Conner smiled shot a laugh out of his nose, "Yah, Mom was kinda hot huh?"

Thoughts of God, church, religion and how to get his

little brother to understand how they all fit together swirled in his head and he was having trouble getting them to sit still long enough to organize the list into a compelling argument.

Ω

Maribelle and her mother had reached the middle of the street.

Ω

It sounded like bad gas. Just like a prolonged bout of abrasive staccato gas bubbling out of some foul orifice. Jesse looked down and rolled his eyes in disgust. Of course the box dolly would have two flat tires. Why wouldn't it? They were both riding on the rims and the flaccid rubber was grinding against the blade as he fought to get the load to move forward.

Annoyance sparked into anger, and as he lowered his shoulder into the metal handle, to begrudgingly force the boxes to inch down the sidewalk, anger erupted into rage. Each time he threw his body into the stack of boxes he added a little more power, and subtracted a little more decorum. He was a few feet from the crosswalk.

Ω

Conner had found a diamond in the rough. A single salient point that he was positive would open Steven's eyes to the real meaning of a relationship with Jesus, and how truly important and urgent that relationship was. A sideways smile brightened his somber demeanor. He opened his mouth to change his brother's life when every feature simply dropped off of his face like he'd been unplugged.

Steven leaned forward, "You okay dude?"

Every hair on Conner's body stood at attention like soldiers in rank and file. A tingle ran up his spine making his eyes water and his nose started to run. Someone must have hit the emergency purge button in his psyche because any remnant of the argument he'd constructed vanished into blackness and was replaced by one simple, powerful thought.

Ω

Thirty years ago, when the city planners who sketched out South Orange County turned to the landscape architects and asked what foliage they suggested to decorate the thoroughfares, there should have been more debate. When a sapling is planted in a blank soil square in the sidewalk, when a city is fresh and new, one must have a forward thinking mindset.

You need to pick a species of tree that does not have an invasive root system. The power that a tree's roots can produce is quite astounding. They can literally move buildings. But the forward minded thinking planner is necessary to foresee the outcome because this power is produced and expelled by the millimeter over decades of growth.

Jesse bent his knees and sprang into the load of boxes for the tenth time. He was less than a foot from the crosswalk. Sweat dripped from his brow and rained down his face in thin beaded streams. Now he had to turn the stubborn conveyance to get it into the street. Perspiration, frustration, fatigue and rage all combined into one final thrust.

He didn't see the woman and her daughter closing the distance to the curb. He didn't hear the little girl singing an original song celebrating her petite stature. He also didn't notice that twenty-nine and a half years ago someone planted a sapling that as a mature tree, now had a root system that branched out in tendrils the width of a healthy boa-constrictor's midsection after a large meal.

The concrete was raised half a foot above the dirt in an

uneven patchwork of happenstance mesas. The lip of the stubbornly flat-tired box dolly caught the slab and sent everything involved, including Jesse tumbling into the street.

Ω

Helplessness and horror fought for dominance in her mind.

"Belly!" Her cry was so frantic and wild, that the last syllable of her verbalized fear came out as more of an animal shriek of terror. She fired out a useless groping hand toward one of those cute, fuzzy tassels that playfully dangled from the collar of her daughter's coat. It closed around empty space as she fell backwards from the force of the young delivery man's shoulder planting firmly in the middle of her chest.

Ω

It wasn't as much of a thought as it was a command. Simple and forceful.

"Get up."

He rose to his feet. There was no debate, no decision. Conner simply obeyed. He had heard that voice before. In a hospital room... in a dream. It was instant. He just knew.

"Go."

As the box connected with the little girl's chest sending her sprawling into the street, he was already moving.

Ω

Natalie was late. She was always late, but this morning she was absurdly late, and not looking forward to hearing about it. She played the scenario out in crystal clarity in her mind, mostly because she'd already lived it to varying degrees before.

Her boss would watch her come in from his glass

encased, fishbowl of an office. He would pop up and look over his computer monitor like a prairie dog checking for danger in some abandoned mid-west corn field, and then slowly turn his bald little head to the left and look at the clock. His eyes would widen, and then with an overly dramatic show of exasperation they would shut. He would then wobble his stout little penguin body out of his chair, out of his office and straight to her desk.

"Forget to set your alarm Ms. Roster?" She mimicked while attempting to trace her eye with liner on, in the rearview mirror.

"No," she said to no one, "I didn't forget. I didn't hear my alarm because my phone doesn't work, because I couldn't charge it, because they cut the power to my apartment yesterday because you don't pay me enough!"

A sip from the warm Diet Coke resting in the cup holder calmed her rage. Lip gloss, brake, mirror, eye shadow, gas, mirror, steer, check the clock, curse, punch the wheel and repeat.

The Starbucks was coming up on her left and she toyed with the possibility of stopping for a latté. Nope, no way she could stop now. If she did, today may be the day her little troll of a boss got the courage to pull the trigger and actually make good on his threats of putting her first in line for unemployment.

As she reached down for another sip of her tepid Diet Coke, her hand bumped the side of the can, sending up a geyser spout of caramel colored liquid over her arm and jeans. Her eyes flicked down to assess the damage.

Ω

Conner always did random off-the-wall things for the pure shock, comedic value of the reaction they elicited. Pant-less Thursdays, how much mustard can I truly fit in my mouth before I vomit, trust fall Tuesdays. So when he popped up, spun and started off into the crosswalk, Steven's first reaction was exasperated amusement.

Confusion quickly replaced humor after Conner's third step hit the ground. He was sprinting. Harder than he should have been for a joke.

Fear shot him out of his seat sending his chair crashing into the window behind their table. The car wasn't slowing down.

"Conner! Car!" He screamed, as he threw the table to the side and headed after his brother into the street.

Ω

There is a portion of the theory of relativity that states, time slows down as one approaches the speed of light. Conner wasn't sure if he was running that fast but it sure felt like it. The world seemed to be stuck in molasses.

His mind raced. It was like his brain had told his adrenal glands to have a going out of business sale… everything must go. Adrenaline tore through his veins fueling him. Senses registered in him at break-neck speed.

The tack of his shoe kissing the pavement. He was very aware of his own breathing. The car was moving so fast. It was a green Dodge Neon. The woman inside had curly brown hair.

Thoughts from his childhood flashed through his mind in a blitzkrieg assault of his past… his life. He could smell the fresh cut grass of the football field the first time he ever set foot on one. He could hear his coach yelling at him to pick up his knees as he ran.

He was five and playing catch with his dad at the park by their house on a Saturday afternoon. He loved his dad so much, he'll understand why, he taught me what it meant to be a man.

He was sitting by the pool next to his dog Alex on a blistering Wednesday in July when he was twelve. It was the day Steven swam the entire length underwater for the first time. He was so excited. He was so proud of his baby brother.

He was going to be a great man… a great father one day. He could hear him screaming somewhere behind him.

His first kiss behind the middle school cafeteria, puppy love, watching the sun sink into the ocean behind Dana Point on a warm spring evening, the taste of his grandmother's cooking, his mother holding him and rocking the fear away when he had a bad dream when was still in diapers. It was his life and he was going to miss it all.

Ω

His right foot scuffed a raised lane marker as he stepped off the curb. Maribelle had sat up and was cradling her bleeding left elbow to her chest as she cried softly for her mommy.

"I've got you…"

One lane.

"Have a family…"

Center of the street.

"Live a good life…"

Nine feet to go.

"Be a good person…."

Tires screamed off to Conner's right as Natalie stood on the brake after looking up from her soda emergency.

Time seemed to stand still. He must have started to hallucinate from all of the adrenaline ravaging his brain but he heard singing. At first it was just a buzzing in his ears, like hearing his pulse rush in his head, but the sound built into something more. It was like someone was turning the dial on an old Ham Radio and finally nailed down the signal.

It was singing, and not just singing but the most powerful, beautiful choir he had ever heard. It resonated through him… he could feel it rattle his bones. It was amazing.

Another footfall, Maribelle had climbed to her knees. Natalie had turned the wheel in a frantic, panicked attempt to avoid disaster. The car had started to skid sideways toward the crosswalk followed closely by a plume of black ash that shot from the melting tires like dragon smoke.

Then there was light. It was brilliant and warm. It simply burst forth from the street, from the air… from around the girl.. It was like someone was slowly opening a door to the sun.

Seven feet…

"Please Jesus… save her," he whispered as he leapt.

The singing swelled and rose to one frenzied beautiful note. He blinked, and for one brief second he saw them. Nods of approval. Mammoth arms holding gargantuan swords were thrown into the air. Flanking him on either side they stood. Huge beautiful beings. Angels… they had to be.

Every fiber in Conner's body strained as he left his feet. Behind him Steven helplessly reached out for his brother and screamed his name. Maribelle's frightened cries mixed with her mother's shrieks of terror, almost matching the high-pitched peel of Natalie's locked tires.

Unheard by anyone but Conner the chorus of angels burst into such a powerful note that he became lost in it. All he could see was the light. There was no pain, no horror. His hands met the crying girl squarely in the middle of her back and sent her tumbling into the arms of her mother who lay on the pavement several feet away.

CHAPTER 8

GLORY IN THE STREET: BEHIND THE VEIL

V. Nicholas Gerasimou

GLORY IN THE STREET: BEHIND THE VEIL

They crawled along the rooftops like agitated ants. Hundreds of them sat on their haunches peering out into the street. Twitching, writhing black wraiths. Insults and profanity shot from their mouths like poison-tipped arrows of hate. Something was going to happen today. Something important.

Sariel stood in front of the coffee shop and calmly surveyed the block. Arms crossed and sword sheathed he stoically tried to count the amassing army of his fallen brethren.

"They certainly are animated toady," he said without looking to Adriel, who stood nearby.

"Indeed," Adriel fluttered his wings and rolled his neck. Anticipation radiated off of him like heat from a raging fire, "It looks as if we may have a busy morning."

Sariel nodded and turned to face his brother in arms, "It makes no difference. The Lord God has blessed me by telling me today is the day my charge will glorify His holy name. Today will start a great movement."

Steven walked up behind Conner and used a full cup of coffee like a door knocker on the back of his brother's head.

Ω

The low hum of insect like chatter on the street was punctuated by the occasional sharp staccato curse or blasphemy of The Lord's name. Each outburst was aimed directly at the small group of Angels surrounding the table where the two boys were having a conversation. It was annoying, but tolerable.

Across the street, a swarm of dark shadows spun like a small tornado around a young man wrestling with a box dolly. They fed frustration into his mind like one drops in kindling before striking the first match. With each shove against the metal frame they sparked the embers of anger into an inferno of rage. Each thrust had more gusto.

The woman and her pretty little daughter were stepping into the crosswalk. From above the yellow striped divide on the opposite side of the street, a hulking dark form emerged from the ranks of demons jostling for position on the roof. It shouldered it's way to the edge of the building and rested a massive scaled hoof just above the rain gutter.

Sariel's hand shot to the hilt of his sword and the five others around him followed suit. From behind him, Gagiel adjusted his scabbard and withdrew his sword a few extra inches so that the sunlight gleamed off of the polished steel and shone into the beast's face.

"Are you trying to antagonize him?" Asked Remiel.

Gagiel let a small smile crack his fierce façade, "Just saying hello."

Ω

Abigor squinted as the light pierced his eyes. His presence was imposing in a physical sense. He stood at least a full body length above most of his counterparts. But his height wasn't what drew the eye, it was his girth.

Abigor simply billowed out from an unseen core somewhere deep within layer upon layer of blubber. Joints were almost indistinguishable from limbs, and where his wide leathery neck ended and his head began was up for debate.

He held up a bulging claw of a hand to shield his lifeless gray eyes from the light, and snorted out a sulfur filled laugh. The girl would die today. She would die badly. It would be on the news, lives would be crushed, souls torn apart and it would be his doing. Let the little band of feathered fools posture all they wanted. There was no stopping what was coming. It was all already in motion.

Ω

Something was wrong. They hadn't made a move. They hadn't attacked. They were waiting for something. Conner was doing what Sariel thought he should have been doing. He was preaching the gospel to his brother. He was going to bring his wayward sibling to know Christ through his testimony. That had to be the plan.

The six holy beings formed a semi-circle around the small circular table and waited. Sariel looked to Adriel and questioned him without saying a word.

"I do not know. All the Lord has revealed to me is that my charge will come to know Him by what his brother does here today," Adriel replied.

Across the street, the swarm of fallen angels had stirred the young delivery man into a frenzy. Directly above the whirlwind of minions, Abigor simply stood watch over the street with a smug satisfaction spread across his drooping jowls that hung from his face like sides of beef in a meat locker.

The woman and her daughter had just crossed the middle of the street.

Abigor slowly turned his head and exhaled a single labored command, "Now."

Instantly, hundreds of evil creatures leapt into the air and momentarily blotted out the sun. The six guardians drew their swords and took defensive positions around the two brothers.

"Protect them at all costs. The Most High commands it!" Sariel yelled to his companions over the sound of a hurricane of demonic wings taking flight.

"Praise be to God!" The five said in unison.

Abigor started to laugh. It was a visible manifestation of demented joy. The chuckle started deep in the heart of his belly and pulsated outward. As his laughter grew in intensity his body began to rhythmically roll and jiggle. It was almost hypnotic.

He let one meaty arm flop out to the left and extended a single talon on it. Sariel followed it with his eyes to a green sedan speeding toward the crosswalk. The car was surrounded by a handful of misshapen shrieking demons.

Sariel's eyes shot from the car, to the little girl skipping across the third lane of traffic with her mother, to the delivery boy who had just cocked back his body like a coiled spring for one final thrust into the stubborn stack of boxes... and finally up to Abigor.

Recognition flashed across the angel's face like lightening. Abigor wanted an audience. When Sariel cried out an alert to his companions, the massive pig-like demon held out his arms in a show of pride as if to welcome everyone in attendance to admire and bask in his handiwork.

The realization of what was occurring dawned on Sariel. He spun to inform his troops when The Most High spoke to him. His face went slack for a moment, then a stern determination chiseled itself into his features.

"Get up." He said with a flat authority.

Adriel turned at the sound of Sariel's voice, "What are you doing?"

Conner turned his head and looked into the street as he rose. Sariel placed a massive powerful hand, lovingly on the boy's back. He knew what was being asked of his charge. The Lord had revealed the entire plan to him for the first time. Then for a moment, there was calm. In the chaos swirling around them, in the space of heartbeat, Sariel and Conner shared a moment.

Conner saw the plan. He knew what he had to do. Sariel showed him the chain reaction playing out in the street and what would happen if he didn't act.

"Go." As he said it, time slammed back into gear.

Conner exploded into the crosswalk like he was running for Olympic Gold, and the line judge had popped the starting pistol.

Abigor saw the boy head into the street and quickly did the math. This could not happen. It would ruin everything. He flung himself down to ground level and barked a frantic command to the cloud of chattering evil hovering above him, "Kill him!"

They immediately descended toward the street like a tidal wave rushing toward a low lying beach front.

Ω

Sariel grabbed Gagiel by the shoulder, "You four take the high ground," a quick motion of his sword informed the three angels standing near Steven, "We will take the low," he said as he pointed at Adriel. "Clear a path for the boy!"

They did not question their commander. They went. Sariel landed in front of Conner and Adriel behind. The two began an ancient dance of death they had perfected before time began. Dodging, parrying, slicing, ducking; they rotated around Conner forming a hedge of violent protection.

Gagiel and his three angelic compatriots simply spun themselves into a blur of blades. It was impossible to identify one single appendage or form, but the carnage that continued to fall in sloppy jagged heaps from above was evidence that the four were doing their job, and doing it well.

Conner had reached the middle of the street, he was footfalls away from the crying girl. The swarm of demons made a last unified push toward the small group in the middle of the street.

Natalie's tires melted away as she slid sideways toward the unseen battle. Jesse slowly pushed himself up from the ground and had a moment to register shocked disbelief at the inevitable catastrophe he'd set in motion. Maribelle turned her head and locked eyes with her mother who was screaming her name, just as Abigor sent his impossible girth into the air.

The world was aimed at Conner, and there were too many for the small band of six to stop.

Then there was light.

Ω

It made the sun seem like a lonely candle set in the middle of a dark room. It was the light of the creator. It erupted from everywhere at once. Blinding and beautiful. Time froze. Sariel blinked and there was peace. The dark army had all simply vanished.

Quietly standing in front of him, in the middle of the street, was The Creator. Behind Him was an entire legion of The Heavenly Host. They filled the sidewalks and alleyways, they lined the rooftops and many of them hovered overhead.

Sariel and the five immediately dropped to their knees. Six sets of eyes cast their gazes to the ground and all thundered in unison, "Praise be to The Lamb! Glory to God most high!"

The Lord slowly walked to where Sariel was knelt. He gently placed a hand on his shoulder and with a motion bid him to rise.

The Lord surveyed the drama that was unfolding before them and turned to Sariel, "You have done well. "

"Thank you Lord," came Sariel's reply dripping with humility and humbleness.

Jesus walked the mighty angel to a spot in front of the boy. Conner was locked in a crouch, about to spring. Effort and determination twisted his face into a mask of what looked like pain. The small girl's tears sat frozen in place on her cheek as she looked to her mother for help, and mere feet away the heat radiating from Natalie's molten right-front tire was shimmering like a small mirage out of the pavement.

The Lord turned to the Holy crowd and said, "My child is about to fulfill a glorious purpose. Rejoice!" A mighty cry of joy erupted from the multitude of angels filling the street. They began to sing.

Emotion tugged at him as he stood in front of Conner. His brothers flanked him on either side, forming an alley of the Heavenly Host. He had been assigned to a countless number of God's children over the millennia. Every one had a specific purpose to fulfill and when their time ended on this Earth he moved on to the next assignment. He cherished and remembered them all, but Sariel was especially proud of this boy.

Time wound back into sync and molecules began to move. Rubber burned, gravel flew and Conner left his feet. In that moment The Lord allowed him to see behind the veil. As the young boy flew through the air the divider between the seen and unseen universe ripped like wet tissue paper.

He blinked and they were simply there. Rank upon rank of mighty glowing being stood cheering for him.

The effort left his face and it was quickly replaced with stunned awe. Conner finally locked eyes with the guardian who had been standing watch over him from the moment of his first breath on Earth until now at his last.

Sariel nodded, Conner closed his eyes and the car passed through the crosswalk.

Ω

An eerie, flat silence settled over the street. It seemed to drop over the scene like a wet blanket muffling out the world. Then one at a time sounds began to register. The tick of Natalie's dying engine picked at the quiet like an impatient child fingers a scab. Her car sat with the rear end edged up on the curb. Maribelle lay cradled in her mother's arms and cried her name over and over again in soft hitching whimpers.

The crowd of onlookers produced an unintelligible mumble that grew in intensity as they processed what they'd just witnessed. Dozens of phones appeared. Some made calls, others started recording.

Steven held his big brother tight to his chest as he slowly rocked back and forth. Short sorrow filled breaths shot out in between sheets of tears. He had to be okay. What in the world had he been thinking? This couldn't be happening. His brother couldn't die... he just couldn't. Fear and panic stole his thoughts and a low hum started to emanate from his throat. It was all he could do. As he rocked the humming became louder and louder until it erupted out of his mouth like a shotgun blast. He screamed into the street, spittle and tears fell from his face like rain.

Unseen by anyone but the eternal, a solitary figure walked from between the standards of angels filling the street. The angels fell to their knees in honor of their King. The man stopped just behind Steven's left shoulder and stood.

He reached out and placed a scarred, worn hand on Conner's forehead and said, "Well done my good and faithful servant. It is time for you to come home my son."

The angels let out a cry of joy from behind him that shook the heavens. Conner's eyes shot open in startled shock. He fought through the haze suffocating his mind and focused. He was there. Standing over his brother's shoulder smiling at him. He looked at his Savior for the first time.

"It's you..." Conner softly exhaled in amazement.

Steven surged at the sound of his brother's voice, "Con! Conner look at me buddy. Are you okay? Can you breathe alright?"

Conner blinked at some of the blood that had pooled in his eye, Steven gingerly wiped it away with the flat of his thumb.

"You just hold on. The ambulance is gonna be here real soon. You hear me? They're going to get you to the hospital and fix you up, okay?" A sob stole his last word.

Conner smiled. It was a smile that Steven had grown up with, known his whole life; familiar. It was a smile that always made him feel safe… loved. It was his big brother's smile.

They looked at each other for a moment, "Hey Con," tears dripped from Steven's cheeks onto Conner's chin as he spoke. He looked so bad. There was so much blood.

Conner looked from his baby brother to his savior, and back again. The Lord softly placed his hands on Steven's shoulders and nodded.

Conner coughed up a throat-full of blood that slid out of the side of his mouth like lava, "The girl?"

Steven stroked his brothers forehead, "She's fine. You got to her."

Conner nodded and then winced as a tremor racked his body. Desperation hijacked Steven's brain. He turned to the mob of bystanders with rage in his eyes, "Call nine-one-one Now! What is wrong with you people? Someone call nine-one-one!"

An elderly man with wire-rimmed glasses and a stout weathered chin covered in graying stubble stepped forward and quietly said, "We've called them son. They're on their way."

Conner's left arm was broken so he used his right to reach up and grab the back of Steven's neck. His liver had been lacerated almost completely in two, his spleen had ruptured and an errant rib had punctured his lung along with the left side of his heart when it shattered. He was bleeding to death from the inside.

"I love you," he said as he pulled Steven's face closer to his own, "I'll see you again okay?"

Steven shook his head as sorrow twisted his face into a mask of pain, "No, no, no, no… don't do that. Please don't. I love you too and you're going to be okay. Stop it."

Conner shook his head in knowing disagreement, and a tear ran down his cheek. His voice squeaked out in a weak whisper, "It's alright. I'm going home now," blood had started to pour out of the corner of his mouth in a thin stream, "I love you Stevie and so does Jesus. Remember that okay? I'll be waiting for you." It was so hard to speak; he could barely fit any air into his lungs now because of all the fluid.

Steven tried to meet Conner's eyes but he kept looking behind him for some reason. Conner smiled again and nodded like someone had said something profound that he agreed with. He rolled his eyes back to his brother's face. Words were impossible, so he squeezed his brother's neck and pulled him close, forehead to forehead.

Conner's eyes fluttered for a moment and then closed. Sorrow crawled up through Steven's chest and poured out of his mouth. His wail disappeared into breathless sobs.

Ω

The Lord placed His hands on Steven's shoulders and whispered in his ear.

Through the whirlwind of agony Steven was caught in, a steady stream of reassurance poured into his soul. It reminded him of what his big brother had done, and what he had died for. From the bottom of the cave of despair, a little voice called to him, it was almost too small to be heard at first, "*I will always be with you,*" it said, "*Believe in me. I will never leave you my child, like I never left your brother.*" Steven heard it.

CHAPTER 9

EPILOGUE: GLORY FULFILLED

V. Nicholas Gerasimou

EPILOGUE: GLORY FULFILLED

The microphone feedback ponged a high-pitched warbled note across the auditorium. The talking slowly dissipated and the attention shifted to the front of the hall. There was a shuffle of papers as Dean Hagar organized himself at the podium. He was a short man but the quiet confidence he carried himself with made him seem taller. As he read his notes he absently swiped a hand across his forehead below his receding hair that was dyed an impossibly deep midnight black.

He settled, adjusted the lapel on his brown tweed coat with a quick tug and began his address, "Good afternoon and welcome to all. My name is Richard Hagar and I have been privileged and blessed to act as Dean of Holy Covenant University for the past eight years."

He set down his notes, took a deep breath and smiled, "In those eight years I've seen thousands of talented, spirited, hard-working young people grow into the world changers that The Lord Jesus had destined them to be. As they walked these halls and attended these classes I've watched them grow and mature from unsure, naive little lambs into the fierce confident lions you see sitting before you today." He made a show of opening his arms in a gesture of observance, identifying the hundreds of students clad in crimson floor length gowns sitting in the rows directly before the stage. He looked like he was trying to take flight.

He let his hands fall and slap to his thighs before he looked back at the audience and continued, "I've seen love, compassion, devotion, and drive from these fine young people. Before I took my seat, a very comfortable leather seat by the way, "Polite laughter softly bounced around the room," As Dean, I was in the classroom. I taught economics for 28 years. As a teacher, your job is to inspire young people by your personality and example. Well, I can tell you that looking at you all today... I am the one who is inspired."

He paused and thoughtfully took a small white note card from his breast pocket. His eyes scanned the list of hastily scratched factoids before he offered himself a small nod of approval and looked up at the room, "As is the custom, we as an administration have chosen a student who exemplifies all of the positive attributes, and characteristics of what we believe a Holy Covenant graduate should be, to deliver the commencement address."

A warm smile spread across his face like a rose slowly opening it's petals to welcome the morning sun, "We have selected a young woman this year who has gone above and beyond in every facet of her collegiate life," he counted on his fingers as he spoke, "academically, spiritually and socially. She's graduating Summa Cum Laude in Business and Religious studies. Last year she self-published a book that has garnished some award recognition detailing her path to faith and the struggles she's faced. On top of that I hear she's a really great cook and has a mean serve on the tennis court." Another ripple of polite laughter danced through the crowd.

He continued, "Ladies and gentlemen, it gives me great pleasure to introduce your two-thousand, twenty eight commencement speaker, Ms. Maribelle Schaefer."

A young woman seated at the far right of the first row of graduates stood and meekly waved to the crowd. She hurriedly skipped up the stairs to the stage propelled by the thunderous applause resonating from behind her.

Dean Hagar shook her hand and Maribelle squared up to the lectern. She absently brushed at a curly stand of auburn hair that had slipped from beneath her cap.

"Thank you Dean Hagar for that introduction. Parents, teachers, friends, family and to all of my peers, hello and good afternoon. It gives me great joy to welcome you to celebrate with the class of twenty twenty-six as we all graduate!" She shook her hands in triumph and an electric smile flashed across her face. Hoots and cat-calls shot back at her from the first few rows, reserved applause rolled in form the back.

She cleared her throat and adjusted the microphone, "Being asked to speak for my entire class and sum up what we've been through and accomplished, and also where we're heading off to, was a huge responsibility that I didn't take lightly. I agonized about what I was going to say and how I was going to say it. I wanted to hit all the beats and yet not be cliché. I wanted to speak about God and yet not preach with a heavy hand. I just wanted this to be good."

"We love you Belly!" someone cried from the crowd. Laughter and few energetic seconds of the sentiment followed before she continued, "Well, I love you too," she said back with a sideways smile.

"I think to truly understand where you're going, you have to understand where you've been. The past four years. The past twelve. Our whole lives. You should all be proud of your accomplishments, and of all of the hard work it took to get here. I know I am." She took a deep breath and closed her eyes. When she opened them she saw her mother. She was sitting in the middle of the crowd and simply beaming. They exchanged a smile and her mom nodded and blew her a kiss.

"I am here because I am driven. Not in a selfish I want to conquer the world kind of a way. I'm driven for a different reason. I have a need to fulfill a life that wasn't lived. It was a life that was given for me, sacrificed for me so that I could continue on."

A tremor of emotion swam through her eyes watering them. "Three months before my fifth birthday I was almost taken from this world. My mother and I were crossing the street and apparently a car lost control and headed for us. I was dead," she paused, "Then from out of nowhere... I wasn't."

Maribelle looked to her mother's right and locked eyes with Steven. He winked and flicked her a quick *thumbs up*. Over the years Conner's brother had become a large part of her life, and a large part of her family.

Ω

After the accident he was numb. It was all a blur of phone calls, hugging, and crying... and the casseroles. There were so many casseroles. At one point he did vividly recollect standing in his parent's kitchen blankly staring at the countertop. There were seven of them. Seven steaming trays of meat-filled sympathy. People just kept bringing them. He didn't know why. Maybe they thought flowers were too cliché.

He didn't remember the planning or preparation for the funeral. Come to think of it, he basically time-traveled through the ceremony as well. To be honest it all kind of seemed like a dream.

Then came the media frenzy. Once the national news networks got a hold of the story of the brave guardian angel who sacrificed himself to save the little girl whom he didn't even know, there was no stopping it. Steven was interviewed so many times he lost track. He fell into a kind of rote routine of reciting the story. It was robotic. There was no emotion or flare, he simply read the lines he'd written for himself and moved onto the next camera lens.

He floated numbly through the following weeks until one weekend he was asked to speak in Conner's church. The same church his big brother had been trying so hard to get him to attend. He agreed and prepared to hit play on the worn out tape recording in his mind again, when he didn't.

He stood at the edge of that stage looking out at those faces and he didn't see what he'd expected. He saw sadness. Genuine sadness and compassion. He also saw a strange pride and love in the hundreds of sets of eyes looking back at him.

This was a huge departure from the ravenous sensationalism he had been brow-beat with over the past few weeks.

Shock stole his voice and he just stood quietly looking at them. He wondered how long they would let this awkward impromptu staring match go on before they pulled the plug and got the hook. Words escaped him and he honestly had no idea what to say.

"It's okay Steven. I know this must be hard," a voice directly behind him softly whispered.

He jumped and turned to see that the Pastor had quietly snuck up during his catatonic vacation.

"Sorry about that," Steven said. He put his hand over the microphone, "You're like a ninja man... you startled me."

The Pastor walked up and put an arm around Steven's shoulders and grabbed the mic with the other. "Thank you for coming today Steven. I can't imagine how difficult this all must be for you. I just want you to know that we all loved your brother very much and we miss him dearly." With that a round of applause made its way through the crowd.

Steven nodded and thanked everyone with a meek wave. The Pastor continued, "I met Conner one fateful night in a back-alley parking lot. He essentially saved my life. It seems he had an affinity for doing that... saving lives." He paused in thought, then continued, "How about this... instead of telling us about that day and what happened, why don't you just tell us about Conner? What was your brother like?"

A warm feeling spread through his neck and stretched his face into a grin. A small chuckle popped out of his mouth before he could choke it down. It was the first time he had smiled in weeks... it felt good. He leaned into the mic, "Stubborn." His description was met with raucous laughter.

"Bullheaded. A prankster. He loved to laugh, mostly at my expense." Then like a river breaching a levy emotion unexpectedly flooded the basin of his brain. His voice dropped a few octaves and the sound of sorrow began to thicken his words. "He was a good man. He loved his family. I know he loved God. The day of the accident he was actually trying to get me to come here. I fought him on it. We were actually bickering about it when it all happened." Steven stopped and let that realization wash over him. His face flushed and tears began to pour down his cheeks.

"I wish he knew I was here now. I wish he knew that I came. I wish he could see."

The Pastor reached over and wrapped Steven in hug. "Trust me he knows, and so does God." Another round of somber applause circled the room. "Let's talk more about how amazing your big brother was, alright?"

They separated and Steven wiped his eyes. With a nod he continued and for the next thirty minutes they celebrated Conner's life. That was the day Steven began his journey. He let a tolerance of God develop into a curiosity. That curiosity blossomed into a relationship, and that relationship changed his life.

That was when he reached out to Maribelle's family. He wanted to know the girl that his brother had died for. In a strange way by having her as a part of his life he felt a connection to Conner. Sixteen years later Uncle Stevie was simply a part of the family.

Ω

Maribelle nodded, "A man I had never met, aside from a wave and a childish giggle minutes before on the sidewalk, sacrificed his life for mine. A man named Conner Parker saved my life that day. He leapt in front of a speeding car and pushed me to safety taking my place in death."

The room was a vacuum of silence, "I said earlier that I am driven. Driven to live my life to its fullest potential to fulfill a life that wasn't lived. Driven to make a man's sacrifice worthwhile. My question for the class of twenty twenty-six is what drives you? We are blessed to attend a university that is based on Christian values and principles. We can talk about God and no one will call the police. I am driven to be the best

I can be because of a man's sacrifice sixteen years ago. But aren't you driven by a sacrifice as well?" She let the question hang in the air for a moment before continuing.

"Two thousand years ago a man died on a cross for all of us. That man was God incarnate. What are you doing to glorify Him for the sacrifice? Good grades? Community service? If you are, that is incredible and I am blessed by it. But think about where we are heading. Out into the world to be the leaders, not of tomorrow, but of today. We can start to change things for the better. Let people see God working through the amazing things we will accomplish out there," with that she shot out her arm like a piston and pointed an excited finger out the window.

"The amazing things that this university has prepared us to do. That God has prepared us to do. I am thrilled at the opportunities ahead of us, and excited to be a part of this journey with all of you. So with that, class of Two-Oh-Two-Six, congratulations to us all… and let's get this show on the road!"

The room vaulted to its feet with applause. Maribelle's mother wiped a tear from her cheek and hugged Steven.

And there on the stage unseen by the crowd, stood a mammoth being. Majestic and terrifying. A glowing holy guardian towered over the girl keeping watch. His hand rested lightly on the hilt of his ancient sword as he surveyed the room. The Lord had great plans for this child of His, and Sariel would protect her.

V. Nicholas Gerasimou

Hidden Steps

V. Nicholas Gerasimou

ABOUT THE AUTHOR

Nick Gerasimou lives in Orange County with his wife and two children. He has been a high school educator for over a decade and currently attends Mariner Mission Viejo Church.

He is also an adviser for the FCA (Fellowship of Christian Athletes) which is a national organization that uses high school sports as a vehicle to share the message of Jesus Christ.

In 2013 he published a topical Bible Study entitled Get up and Walk: A Stroll With Jesus. All of his works are available on Amazon.

Hidden Steps

Made in the USA
San Bernardino, CA
08 December 2014